DDR limited

THE SPECIAL LIFE

AND STYLE AT

STRAUSBERGER PLATZ,

KARL-MARX-ALLEE

IN EAST BERLIN

DDR limited

ÜBER DAS LEBEN UND

WOHNEN AM

STRAUSBERGER PLATZ,

KARL-MARX-ALLEE

IN OSTBERLIN

STEPHAN SCHILGEN, ANDRÉ M. WYST

PROLOGUE / PROLOG

Strausberger Platz: Stuck in Stalinist Empire Architecture or Representing Modern Variety? – Considering its almost inexplicable proximity to the city's center, this vast lane that cuts through the city, towards the rising sun, dead straight and as broad as a space shuttle's landing strip, seems strange to the newcomer at first. It all comes down to Berlin's crazy history, the destruction of the city, the separation and the reconstruction beginning in 1945. Here, the bombings in World War II, destroyed almost all of the buildings and under the ruins and rubble a vast space where the new ruling class, not having to consider private property, were able to implement their own ideas on a grand scale. There was to be a pompous boulevard, following the Soviet examples: the Stalinallee.

In the end, there was a wild but yet harmonious mixture of architectural styles. Historicist and modern components were implemented with the typical German perfectionism of that era, never minding the so called "supply bottlenecks". The association with American skyscrapers, like the Municpal Building in New York City or the Civic Opera House of Chicago, is not a coincidence. It was indeed a gigantic project, which would not have been possible without the spirit of optimism that had arisen from the end of the war and the founding of the state in 1949. 40,000 workers cleared away the rubble that was left after the destruction. From this rubble they erected housing blocks with up to 13 floors, of which there were no precedences in the city. Only in Moscow, on top of the Lenin Hills, one could find these oddly Gothic seeming blocks, known as the "Seven Sisters". However, whereas the Soviets left the buildings unplastered and used them as Ministry of Foreign Affairs, Hotel Ukraina or Lomonosov Moscow State University, the Germans plastered their ribbon development with textured majolica tiles made of Meissen porcelain which gave a lightness to its overall appearance. This lightness was refined by adding Venetian colonnades and in the end, the copy was better than the original.

This new German style of a "National Tradition" could do without all the overblown pathos, mainly because of the gigantomaniac transgressions of the hardly overcome war. Yet it stayed true to its diversity and playfulness, functional in its exposure and as far as possible, true to the Bauhaus movement. This is due in great part to chief architects Hermann Henselmann and Richard Paulick. Henselmann was of Jewish heritage and thus unrecognised during the Nazi period. He was a giant born among the likes of Speer and Eiermann who was also gifted with a knack for urban planning. In 1949 he was already appointed to the GDR Academy of Science and developed his own architectural ideas of social realism. The game-changing apartment tower at Weberwiese was Henselmann's design and if it had been up to him, he would have built all of Stalinallee in this style. But Moscow had other ideas, namely to recreate the Soviet gingerbread style. During the so-called "anti-formalism debate" at the beginning of the 1950s, the Stalinist German SED leaders (Socialist Unity Party) also attempted to discourage the architects from repeating the alleged decadent Western Bauhaus tradition.

The development of this project of the century is to be considered between the conflicting priorities of political standards and anarchically individual creativity. One can claim quite rightly that the present day Karl-Marx-Allee and the Strausberger Platz in their compactness are the greatest thing in building history the GDR has produced. Not just since it had been declared a monument (exactly one day before the political turnaround on November, 9th 1989) its diversity of styles is regarded as unique, but the nomination as a UNESCO cultural heritage site confirms this internationally. DDR Limited, the volume on hand, goes beyond in terms of content. It will reveal just how groundbreaking this kind of architecture is, even today. It will show how tasteful contemporaries have gratefully made themselves at home in these timeless ergonomic rooms and how one can perfectly integrate modern furnishing ideas into these living quarters. The ambience is completed by additional innovations of mid-century GDR. It is time that groundbreaking designs finally receive recognition and acknowledgement. They are contemporary witnesses of an all-German past and its consequent Eastern design movement. On top of the housing options, they illustrate how thoroughly fascinated and inspired we are by this comparatively short period of time.

This volume includes scents from Strausberger Platz in 1950 and today. The scent scientist Sissel Tolaas leads us to the difference.

◇◇◇◇◇◇

Strausberger Platz: Starre Stalin-Gotik oder Vielfalt der Moderne? – Diese Schneise durch die große Stadt, der aufgehenden Sonne entgegen, gerade wie eine Schnur und breit wie eine Landebahn, wirkt auf den Neuankömmling zunächst fremdartig und in ihrer City-Nähe kaum erklärbar. Verständlich wird alles erst durch die verrückte Geschichte Berlins, die Zerstörung einer Stadt, ihre Teilung und den Wiederaufbau ab 1945. Hier standen nur noch wenige Häuser, fast alles war zerbombt worden. Unter dem Schutt gab es eine Menge Platz; die neuen Herrschenden konnten, ohne Rücksicht auf Privateigentum im großen Stil planen und es sollte ein Prachtboulevard nach sowjetischem Vorbild entstehen: die Stalinallee.

Am Ende rahmte diese Allee ein wilder und doch harmonisch anmutender Stilmix aus modernen und Historismus-Komponenten, trotz der sogenannten Versorgungsengpässe umgesetzt mit dem typisch deutschen Perfektionismus jener Jahre. Die Assoziation zu amerikanischen Hochhäusern, wie dem Municipal Building in New York oder dem Opernhaus in Chicago ist nicht zufällig.

Es war ein gigantisches Projekt, das ohne die Aufbruchstimmung nach dem Krieg und die Staatsgründung der DDR 1949 nicht möglich gewesen wäre. 40.000 Arbeiter beseitigten mit ihren Händen den Schutt und errichteten im Akkord bis zu 13-geschossige Wohnblöcke, für die es in Berlin kein Vorbild gab. Nur in Moskau ragten jene bizarr gotisch anmutenden Mammutblöcke der „Sieben

Schwestern" empor, auf den Leninbergen und in der Stadt verteilt. Doch während die Sowjets ihre Hochbauten, darunter das Außenministerium, das „Hotel Ukraine" und die Lomonossow-Universität unverputzt ließen, verkleideten die Deutschen ihre Zeilenblöcke mit reliefierten, handgefertigten Fliesen aus Meissen und gaben so deren gesamter Erscheinung jene Leichtigkeit, welche durch luftig-venezianische Kollonadenkronen noch veredelt wurde: Die Kopie war am Ende besser als das Original.

Dieser neue deutsche Stil der „Nationalen Tradition" entbehrte allem schwülstigen Pathos, auch als Folge der gigantomanischen Verfehlungen des gerade Überwundenen, und blieb doch vielfältig und verspielt, in seiner Exponiertheit sachlich und, soweit es ging, der Bewegung des Bauhaus verbunden. Dies war vor allem den Chefarchitekten Hermann Henselmann und Richard Paulick zu verdanken. Henselmann, ab 1940 als sogenannter Halbjude kaum tätig, war ein mit dem stadtplanerischem Gen ausgestatteter Architekt aus der Generation der Speers und Eiermanns. Bereits 1949 berufen in die Akademie der Wissenschaften der DDR, entwickelte er seine Architekturvorstellung vom Sozialistischen Realismus, entwarf das wegweisende Hochhaus an der Weberwiese und wollte die gesamte Stalinallee danach bebauen. Aus Moskau kamen jedoch Anweisungen, den Sowjetischen Zuckerbäckerstil zu übernehmen und auch die stalinistische deutsche SED-Führung versuchte in der sogenannten Antiformalismusdebatte gleich zu Anfang der 50er Jahre, ihn und die anderen beteiligten Architekten von der angeblich westlich-dekadenten Bauhaus-Tradition abzubringen.

In diesem Spannungsfeld aus politischen Vorgaben und anarchisch-individueller Kreativität ist die Bebauung des Jahrhundert-Projektes zu sehen. Und man kann mit Fug und Recht behaupten, dass die heutige Karl-Marx-Allee mit dem Strausberger Platz in seiner Kompaktheit das Größte ist, was die DDR bauhistorisch hervorgebracht hat. Ihre Vielfalt der Stile gilt nicht erst seit der Ernennung zum Denkmal - einen Tag vor der politischen Wende am 9.11.1989 – als einmalig; die aktuell laufende Bewerbung um Auszeichnung als UNESCO-Weltkulturerbe bestätigt dies auch international.

Der vorliegende Band „DDR Limited" geht inhaltlich aber weiter. Er wird aufzeigen, wie wegweisend jene Architektur noch heute ist, wie dankbar sich stilbewusste Zeitgenossen verschiedenster Couleur in den zeitlos-ergonomischen Raumschnitten eingerichtet haben und wie perfekt jene Wohneinheiten auch moderne Einrichtungsideen integrieren. Komplettiert werden die Ambientes durch weitere Innovationen des DDR-Midcentury. Wegweisende Designs sollen hier Erwähnung finden, als Zeitzeugen jener aus gesamtdeutscher Vergangenheit erwachsenen Designbewegung des Ostens. Neben den Wohnbeispielen illustrieren sie, wie gründlich uns jener kurze Abschnitt der Geschichte noch heute faszinieren und inspirieren kann.

Dieser Band ist mit Gerüchen vom Strausberger Platz 1950 und heute imprägniert. Die Geruchswissenschaftlerin Sissel Tolaas erklärt uns den Unterschied.

STEPHAN SCHILGEN

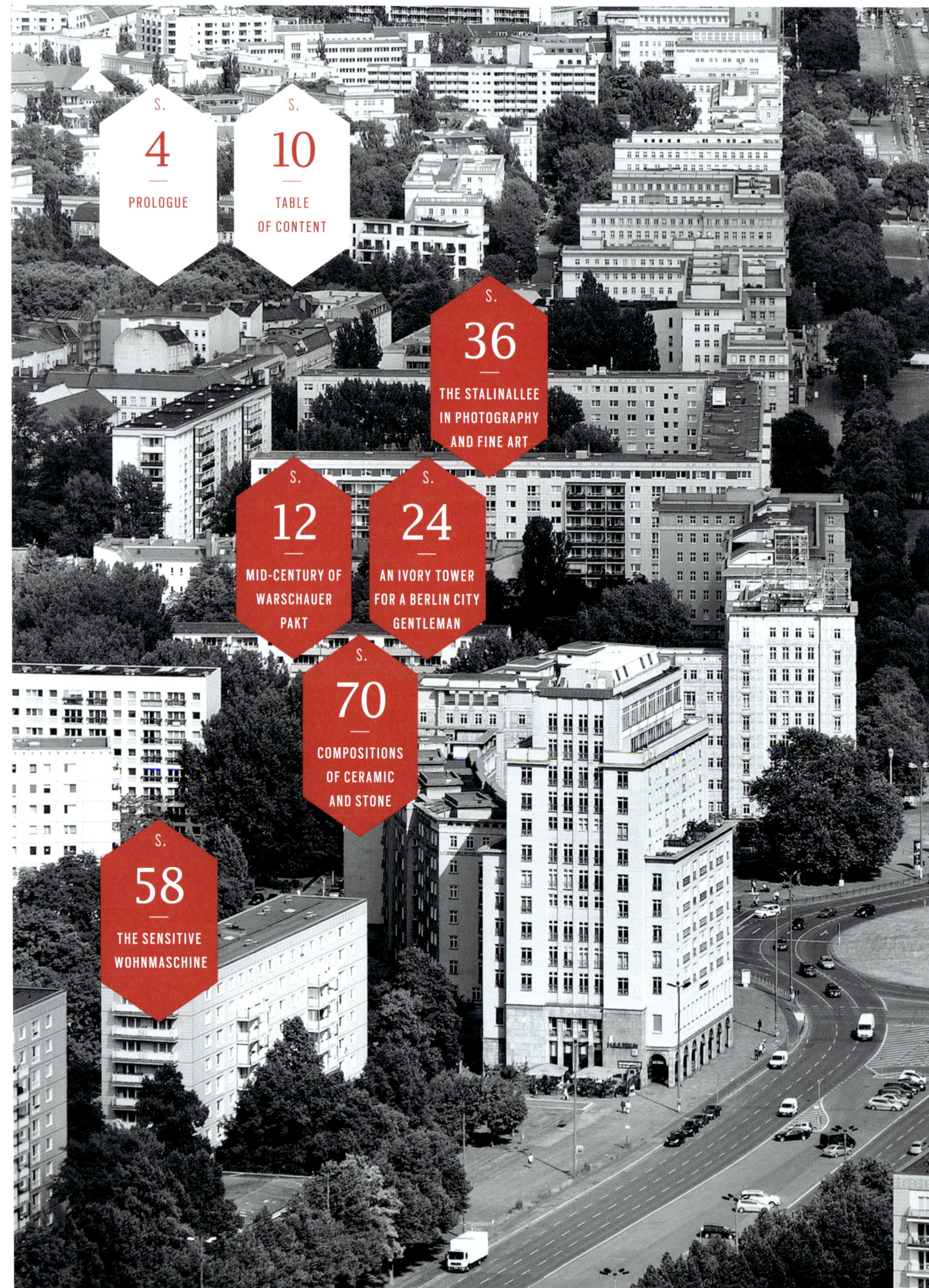

- S. 4 — PROLOGUE
- S. 10 — TABLE OF CONTENT
- S. 12 — MID-CENTURY OF WARSCHAUER PAKT
- S. 24 — AN IVORY TOWER FOR A BERLIN CITY GENTLEMAN
- S. 36 — THE STALINALLEE IN PHOTOGRAPHY AND FINE ART
- S. 58 — THE SENSITIVE WOHNMASCHINE
- S. 70 — COMPOSITIONS OF CERAMIC AND STONE

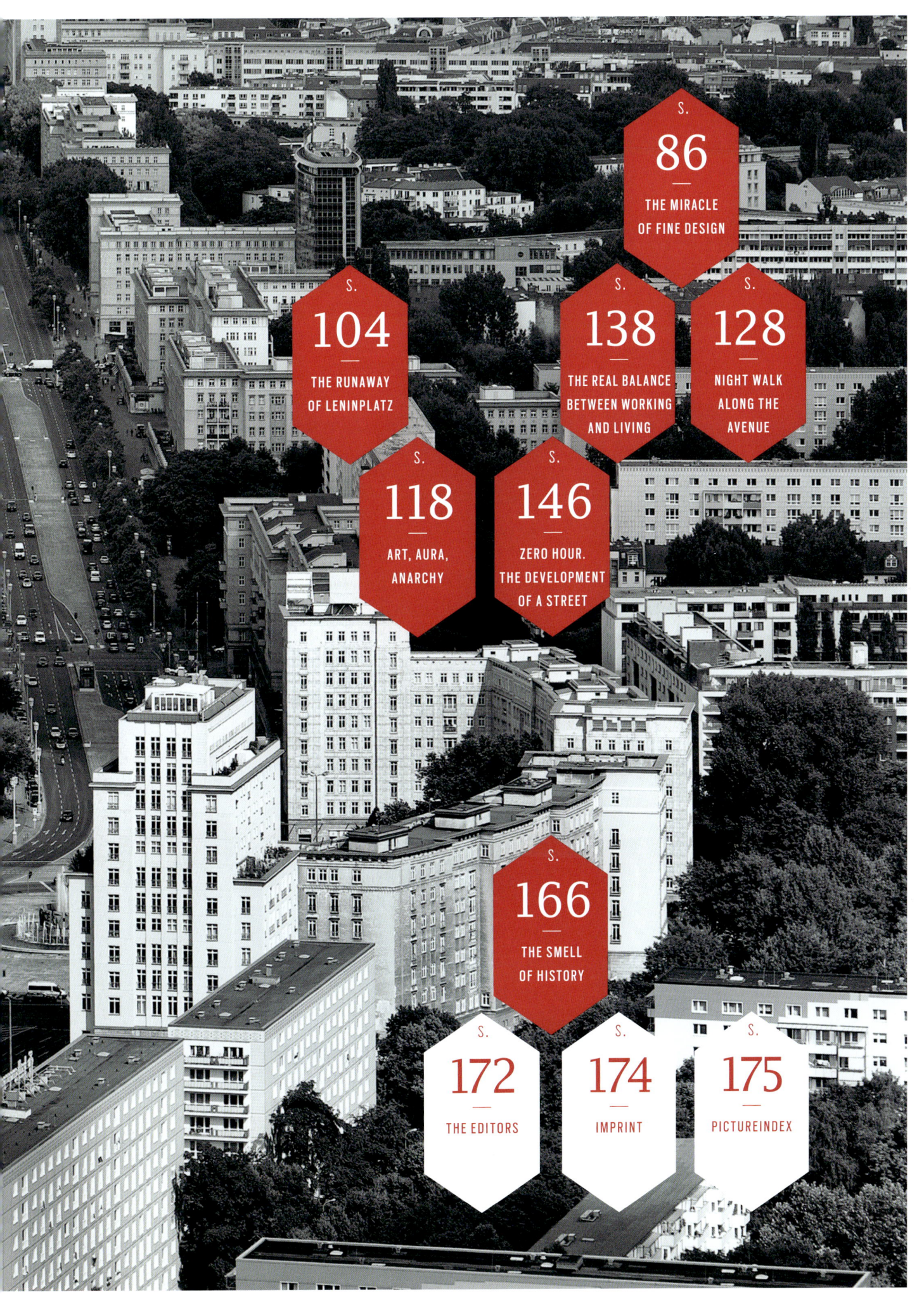

- S. 86 — THE MIRACLE OF FINE DESIGN
- S. 104 — THE RUNAWAY OF LENINPLATZ
- S. 138 — THE REAL BALANCE BETWEEN WORKING AND LIVING
- S. 128 — NIGHT WALK ALONG THE AVENUE
- S. 118 — ART, AURA, ANARCHY
- S. 146 — ZERO HOUR. THE DEVELOPMENT OF A STREET
- S. 166 — THE SMELL OF HISTORY
- S. 172 — THE EDITORS
- S. 174 — IMPRINT
- S. 175 — PICTUREINDEX

MID-CENTURY OF WARSCHAUER PAKT

A COMMUNIST UTOPIA AND FURNITURE FROM THE WEST: DO THEY MATCH? YES, VERY WELL INDEED – *EINE KOMMUNISTISCHE UTOPIE UND WESTLICHE MÖBEL: PASST DAS ZUSAMMEN? SEHR GUT SOGAR*

PHOTOS: OLIVER MARK

Composition of colours ties surfaces with furniture. Auböck coffee table and Roland Rainer chairs reference the warmth of the parquet flooring; their stands mirror the anthracite grey of the curtains and the Borsani Lounger. The DW 112 table by Helmut Magg perfects the reduction to black/white/brown.

—

Komponiertes Farbenspiel verbindet Oberflächen mit Möbeln. Der Auböck-Couchtisch und die Stühle von Roland Rainer referieren die Wärme des Parketts, ihre Gestelle nehmen das Anthrazit der Vorhänge und des Loungers von Borsani auf. Der Tisch DW 112 von Helmut Magg komplettiert die Reduktion auf Schwarz-Weiß-Braun.

Lying on the plywood daybed from 1953 looking up at the mystical romantic painting "Neuschwanstein III" (2005) by Armin Boehm truly makes you dream. Later on, you can read the newspaper under the Pilastro floor lamp of the same period while the Aalto stool functions as a side table for tea and biscuits.
—
Vor dem 2005 entstandenen, mystisch-romantischen Gemälde „Neuschwanstein III" von Armin Boehm lässt es sich träumen – idealerweise liegend auf dem Schichtholz-Daybed von 1953. Unter der ebenso alten Pilastro-Stehleuchte kann man danach Zeitung lesen; der Aalto-Hocker dient als Tee und Gebäck tragendes Beistelltischchen.

25 years later: reunification between icons from East and West. The iconic desk from the Saxon Deutsche Werkstätten Hellerau workshops of the GDR, designed as "Typ 602" by Franz Ehrlich, now shines beside Artflex´ "Lady"-Chair, an achievement of the former so-called capitalist foreign countries.

—

Nach 25 Jahren: Wiedervereinigung von Ost- und West-Ikonen. Der kultige Schreibtisch aus den Deutsche Werkstätten Hellerau in Sachsen, entworfen als „Typ 602" von Franz Ehrlich, glänzt neben dem „Lady"-Sessel von Artflex / Italy, einer Errungenschaft aus dem ehemaligen „kapitalistischen Ausland".

The sixth floor at Strausberger Platz, approximately 100 sqm. A spacious hallway with glass doors leads to two elongated rooms with an adjacent third room. All windows face the square and its round fountain. The herringbone parquet in the living areas is of aged Siberian spruce in a warm brown colour, all heaters are panelled in German Bauhaus style. The Stalin's Empire stucco functions also as a frame for the rigid curtains that at the end of a long day veil the view onto the square and its prospect.

A visitor's first impression: a pleasant set-up, the walls and doors seem to be in the right place. Were there any alterations in substance? No, the interior designer kept the original floorplan, interchanging merely kitchen and bedroom to give the only room facing the rear of the house a contemporary functionality. With its brilliant simplicity, this layout is an ideal blueprint for chic furniture of any decade. In this case, the owner chose to stay true to the period, creating a nostalgic sense of authenticity in style, which is rare enough to find.

Gradually, it becomes more obvious that the furniture from the other side of the political map integrates very harmoniously with the former GDR apartment. An endearing sign for the closeness of the two movements that were to some extent competing already in the fifties, even though its protagonists were partly the same.

And these are not the only overlaps. The door installation "We Pass Through This" by Martin Boyce right at the entrance is a respectable retro component. This site-specific installation seems to be modelled on a pattern of cloth, despite its metallic stiffness. With its wonderfully displayed fractured geometric forms it serves no other function than to subtly pay homage to that period. The kitchen is a functional black floating monolith with custom-made brass gratings as precious flashing details. It is obvious that the main intention is not a contrasting but an integrational use of matter. Well done! This is the work of a sentimental artist, not an iconoclast.

◇◇◇◇◇◇

Sechster Stock am Strausberger Platz, knapp 100 Quadratmeter. Eine großzügige quadratische Diele, deren verglaste Türen zu zwei länglichen Zimmern führen, ein dritter Raum liegt daneben. Alle Fenster gehen auf den Platz mit seinem runden Wasserspiel in der Mitte hinaus. Die Böden der Wohnräume bedeckt Fischgrätparkett aus gealterter, warmbrauner sibirischer Fichte, alle Heizkörper sind im Bauhaus-Stil vertäfelt. Der Stalin-Empire-Stuck dient unter anderem als Blende für die strengen Vorhänge, mit denen sich am Ende eines langen Tages die Sicht auf den Platz und seinen Prospekt verhüllen lassen.

Erster Eindruck des Besuchers: angenehme Raumordnung, Wände und Türen gefühlt an der richtigen Stelle. Wurde hier substanziell eingegriffen? Nein, der Interior Designer ließ den alten Grundriss bestehen, tauschte lediglich Schlafzimmer und Küche, um dem einzigen ruhigen Zimmer nach hinten zeitgemäße Funktion zu geben, und beließ den Rest beim Alten. In seiner genialen Schlichtheit dient der Grundriss als ideale Blaupause für den Genuss schicker Möbel jedweder Epoche; in diesem Fall hat sich der Eigentümer für das zeitlich Adäquate entschieden, was das befriedend nostalgische Gefühl vermittelt, in Stilechtheit zu wandeln – ein seltener Umstand.

Mit jedem Schritt spürt man mehr, wie harmonisch sich gerade das Mobiliar von der anderen Seite der politischen Landkarte in die einstige DDR-Wohnung einschmiegt, ein liebenswertes Zeichen für die geschwisterliche Nähe, in der sich die teils bereits konkurrierenden Bewegungen in den 50er-Jahren befanden, wiewohl deren Protagonisten zum Teil dieselben waren.

Und es zeigen sich weitere Überraschungen. Als seriöse Retrokomponente erkennt man gleich beim Eintritt die Blendentüre „We Pass Through This" von Martin Boyce, ein Piece als „site specific installation", wie einem Stoffmuster nachempfunden und gleichsam metallisch erstarrt, mit wundervoll inszenierten, geometrisch gebrochenen Referenzen an jene Zeit, der sie hintergründig-zweckfrei huldigt. Auch der monolithische, scheinbar schwebende Küchenblock in Schwarz und die als wertvolle Details aufblitzenden, eigens kreierten Lüftungsgitter aus Messing wollen nicht Bestehendes kontrastieren, sondern zeugen von liebevoll verbindendem Umgang mit der Materie. Hier wollte sich in der Tat ein sentimentalischer Künstler ausleben, kein Bilderstürmer.

This "Iron Curtain" offers at least a fractured privacy shield against entrants, while playing with the function of its textile predecessors and might even be happy about being misused as a coat rack.

—

Dieser „Eiserne Vorhang" bietet zumindest gebrochenen Sichtschutz gegen Eintretende, spielt zweckfrei mit der Idee seiner textilen Vorgänger und freut sich irgendwann über den Missbrauch als Garderobe.

The coffering of the doors is typical for the Socialist Classicism style of the period while, intentionally or no, the door handle is pure Bauhaus. The high-gloss herringbone parquet gives the room its finishing touch.

—

Die Kassettierungen der Türen sind typisch für den sozialistischen Klassizismus jener Zeit, die Türklinke bleibt – zufällig oder gewollt – reinstes Bauhaus. Hochglänzendes Fischgrätparkett veredelt den Raum.

"Slow and everywhere like breath" the five words of this sentence are spread throughout the rooms' brass gratings as components of the poetic description of their original purpose. On the right side is the floating kitchen unit.

—

„Slow and everywhere like breath": Die Worte dieses Satzes verteilen sich auf die fünf Lüftungsgitter aus Messing in den Räumen, als Bausteine poetischer Beschreibung der eigentlichen Bestimmung. Rechts die scheinbar schwebende Küche.

AN IVORY TOWER FOR A BERLIN CITY GENTLEMAN

360 DEGREE VIEW, 100 STEPS UP, 2 TOWERS AND ONE HAPPY RESIDENT — *360 GRAD RUNDUMBLICK, 100 TREPPENSTUFEN, 2 TÜRME UND EIN GLÜCKLICHER BEWOHNER*

PHOTOS: OLIVER MARK

A look around the varied mix of furniture styles and accessories onto the historicising architecture. Note the concentric inlay on the floor bearing a Soviet star.

—

Blick über den bunten Stilmix an Möbeln und Accessoires auf historisierende Architektur. Man beachte das konzentrische Bodenintarsium mit Sowjetstern.

Colonades and circular stairs, black linoleum, handrails and banisters girded in style-defining blue glass tubes: pure Fifties.

—

Wandelgänge und Wendeltreppen, schwarzes Linoleum und Handläufe auf Geländerstäben, deren umgürtende Blauglashülsen den Stil prägen: pure Fifties.

The corner of Karl-Marx-Allee and Warschauer Straße, 30 metres above one of the city's busiest intersections: Here stand the twin towers like an emphasis, the peak of the whole ensemble. Just a few years ago, an apartment was built into the dome of one of the towers.

After the elevator reaches the 10th floor, it takes another 100 steps up to the dome hall that impresses with its 12 metre height. The wraparound tall windows offer a spectacular 360 degree view. A double door opens onto the balcony that encircles the tower. The gaze reaches beyond the Berlin TV tower – which is inspired by Henselmann – to the 20s Funkturm far away in Charlottenburg-Westend. In the distance you can spot departing and landing airplanes from Tegel or Schönefeld Airport. If you are lucky you will even find a falcon resting among the roof beams above – a noble symbol of urban history.

This hideaway encompasses three storeys, each 40 sqm. An additional elevator has been built recently, leading directly into the kitchen which was just barely approved by the heritage preservation authority. The rotunda is made of a subtle yellow stone. Between the metal window hinges classic wall lamps form a circle of light. It truly is a challenge to fit furniture into the space, but the chesterfields work and antique stuffed animals contribute to an exotic and unique look. A different kind of place indeed, not only because preparing a sunday breakfast includes several trips up and down the three floors. Besides the tower's twin almost within arm's reach nothing disturbs this unique view. It is an other-worldly feeling, storms are more capturing here and sunsets seem metaphysical and inspire those lucky and privileged enough to witness them from up here.

◇◇◇◇◇

Karl-Marx-Allee Ecke Warschauer Straße stehen, als spannender Akzent das gesamte Ensemble pointierend, Zwillings-Turmhäuser, deren eine pantheonartig entrückte Säulenkuppel tatsächlich seit einigen Jahren bewohnt ist. Sie thront 30 Meter über einer der am meisten befahrenen Kreuzungen der Stadt.

Mit dem Fahrstuhl geht es ins zehnte Stockwerk, von dort weitere 100 Stufen hinauf in den zwölf Meter hohen Kuppelsaal, dessen fast raumhohe Fenster einen fulminanten Rundumblick über Berlin bieten. Durch eine Flügeltür gelangt man auf den umlaufenden Balkon, von hier aus kann der Blick vorbei am Fernsehturm bis zum Funkturm im Westend schweifen; startende und landende Flugzeuge von Schönefeld und Tegel sind zu sehen, manchmal auch ein Turmfalke im Gebälk als edles Sinnbild urbaner Geschichte.

Das Refugium erstreckt sich über drei Stockwerke à 40 Quadratmeter, ein zweiter Fahrstuhl führt neuerdings sogar bis hoch in die Küche, deren Einbau das Denkmalamt gerade so freigegeben hat. Möbel passen kaum hinein, aber das ist ja die Herausforderung. Die Chesterfield-Sofas funktionieren in ihrer Konstellation, historische Tierpräparate und Felle exotisieren den Spot und erheben ihn weiter ins Solitäre. Es ist halt sehr anders hier, und zur Fertigstellung des sonntäglichen Frühstücks hat man die Etagen bereits mehrfach überwunden. Aber bis auf den Zwillingsturm in greifbarer Nähe steht nichts im Weg. Die Aussicht ist einmalig, man fühlt sich entrückt, Stürme und Gewitter ergreifen, Sundowner wirken metaphysisch und inspirieren jenen, der die Ehre und das Vergnügen hat, hier sein zu dürfen.

The view onto the opposite twin tower in the style of the Greek Pantheon is like a look in the mirror.

—

Wie in einen Spiegel blickt man auf den ans griechische Pantheon erinnernden Zwillingsturm gegenüber.

A hodge podge of old biological displays indicate the resident's collector's passion. A near and dear tower view over the green city.

—

Ein Sammelsurium alter biologischer Schaukästen zeugt von der Sammelleidenschaft des Citoyens. Teurer Turmblick über die grüne Stadt.

Like the digits on a clock-face, the seats on the balcony represent the omnipresent concentric order that is so pleasant to the eye.
—
Allgegenwärtige Konzentrik strahlt angenehm ordnend auf die Sinne. Die Logenplätze des Balkon wirken wie Ziffern auf einer Uhr.

THE STALINALLEE IN PHOTOGRAPHY AND FINE ART

THE OUTSTANDING BUILDINGS AND ENSEMBLES OF THE KARL-MARX-ALLEE STILL STIMULATE AND INSPIRE ARTISTS EVEN TODAY – *IHRE HERAUSRAGENDEN GEBÄUDE UND ENSEMBLES ANIMIEREN KÜNSTLER BIS HEUTE, SICH MIT DER KARL-MARX-ALLEE ZU BESCHÄFTIGEN*

HARALD HAUSWALD, MAX ITTENBACH, PRESSE FOTO RÖHNERT, THOMAS SANDBERG, WALTER WOMACKA UND LUDWIG SCHIRMER

MAX ITTENBACH, 1960
Car parade of olympic athletes at Stalinallee
—
Autokorso Olympischer Athleten auf der Stalinallee

HARALD HAUSWALD, 1984
International Labor Day of
the working class, Karl-Marx-Allee

—

*Internationaler Kampftag der
Arbeiterklasse, Karl-Marx-Allee*

HARALD HAUSWALD, 1985
Young Student
at Strausberger Platz

—

*Junger Student
am Strausberger Platz*

PRESSEFOTO RÖHNERT, CA. 1960
Strausberger Platz
with Lufthansa obelisk

—

*Strausberger Platz mit
Lufthansa obelisk*

MAX ITTENBACH, 1955
Juice bar on a hot summer day, Stalinallee

—

Saftausschank an einem heißen Sommertag, Stalinallee

WALTER WOMACKA, 1961
Construction of Karl-Marx-Allee,
Watercolor
The old substance shown on this picture had to make way for the new buildings.

*Aufbau der Karl-Marx-Allee,
Aquarell
Schön zu sehen ist hier noch
die alte Bausubstanz, die neuen
Häusern weichen musste.*

LUDWIG SCHIRMER, CA. 1955

Exploration through the
windshield, Frankfurter Tor

—

Erkundung durch die
Frontscheibe, Frankfurter Tor

PETER M. OLSEN, CA. 1955

Flagged facade observed
through the rear side window

—

Beflaggte Fassade durchs hintere
Seitenfenster observierend

45

MAX ITTENBACH, CA. 1970
Interflor Blumenhaus
(flower shop), Karl-Marx-Allee 32

—

Interflor Blumenhaus,
Karl-Marx-Allee 32

MAX ITTENBACH, CA. 1960
Milk Bar Mokka-Milch-Eisbar,
Karl-Marx-Allee 35

—

Mokka-Milch-Eisbar,
Karl-Marx-Allee 35

UNKNOWN, CA. 1958
Café Warschau,
Karl-Marx-Allee 93a

—

Café Warschau,
Karl-Marx-Allee 93a

UNKNOWN, CA. 1958
Restaurant Budapest,
Karl-Marx-Allee 91

—

Gaststätte Budapest,
Karl-Marx-Allee 91

51

HEINRICH WITZ, 1953

May 1st Rally Stalinallee

—

*Erste-Mai-Kundgebung
Stalinallee*

HARALD HAUSWALD, 1989

Fountain of Friendship between
Peoples, Alexanderplatz

—

Brunnen der Völkerfreunschaft,
Alexanderplatz

HARALD HAUSWALD, 1989

Pavillon Kunst im Heim,
Karl-Marx-Allee 45

—

Pavilion Kunst im Heim,
Karl-Marx-Allee 45

HARALD HAUSWALD, CA. 1990
Demonstration at Frankfurter Allee
—
Aufmarsch an der Frankfurter Allee

THOMAS SANDBERG, 1977
Erich Honecker, May 1st at Karl-Marx-Allee, Employees of the Ministry for State Security in tracksuits carrying pictures of the politburo
—
Erich Honecker, 1. Mai auf der Karl-Marx-Allee, Mitarbeiter des MfS in Trainingsanzügen tragen die Bilder des Politbüros

MAX ITTENBACH, CA. 1965

(clockwise) Customers at Café Moskau, Karl-Marx-Allee 34. Terrace of Café Warschau, Karl-Marx-Allee 93a. Showroom at the studio of arts and crafts, Karl-Marx-Allee

—

(v.l.n.r.) Gäste im Café Moskau, Karl-Marx-Allee 34. Terrasse Café Warschau, Karl-Marx-Allee 93a. Schauraum des Kunstgewerbeateliers, Karl-Marx-Allee.

THE SENSITIVE ´WOHNMASCHINE´

WHAT HAPPENS WHEN LIVING SPACE REINVENTS ITSELF VIA A PINK CABINET TENDRIL – *WAS GESCHIEHT, WENN SICH WOHNRAUM DURCH EINE ROSA SCHRANK-RANKE NEU ERFINDET*

PHOTOS: ANDREAS GERKE

From the first look into the open apartment the message is clear: "Follow the pink surfaces". But upon entering, the golden shrine, like a mysterious altar, captivates and distracts us.

—

Bereits der erste Blick in die offene Wohnung macht klar: „Folgen Sie den rosa Flächen". Doch beim Eintreten zieht uns der goldene Schrein wie ein rätselhafter Altar in seinen Bann und will ablenken.

To the left into the bedroom or, passing the kitchen unit, to the right into the living room: The omnipresent pink "Wohnmaschine" and the dark brown oiled herringbone parquet throughout the rooms form a stylish entity.

—

Nach links ins Schlafzimmer oder nach rechts, vorbei an der Küchenzeile, ins Wohnzimmer: Neben der allgegenwärtigen rosa Wohnmaschine verbindet das dunkelbraun geölte Fischgrätparkett die Räume zur stilsicheren Einheit.

De luxe bed-chamber: Artemide desk lamp and Minotti carpet, the Art Deco bed topped by a throw with floral op art pattern in the same confident color spectrum. The "Wohnmaschine" as the functional dominant is always present.

—

Schlafgemach de luxe: Tischleuchte von Artemide und Minotti-Teppich. Das Art déco-Bett umschmeichelt der Überwurf mit floralem Op-Art-Muster, alles im selbstbewusst gesetzten Farbspektrum. Als funktionale Dominante ist die Wohnmaschine stets anwesend.

The functional spaces form a line and allow a chain of communication from the bathtub into the smallest corner of the apartment. Here taking a bath while someone else is cooking is a must, meanwhile discussing recipes or the benefits of a long hot bubble bath.

—

Aufgereihte Funktionsräume ermöglichen Kettenkommunikation aus der Wanne bis in den kleinsten Winkel des Apartments. Hier muss man ein Bad nehmen, während jemand kocht, und sich mit demjenigen über Rezepte unterhalten - oder über die Vorteile des langen Heißschaumbadens.

Rumor has it that the interior designers of this unusual apartment were asked to include no other furniture but a table and a bed. Instead of cupboards and shelves, a light pink, metastatic built-in shelving system made of closed tanks has been installed, even at the risk of looking monotonous. The fact that an armchair and a bar stool also found their way inside does not negate this resolute decision. Flush-mount veneered the tank system clings hermetically elegant to the walls throughout the rooms and puts everything in relation to itself. Only the kitchen unit is fitted with laterally open shelves. Merely the golden cavity interrupts the system, forming an exception and an exotic break compared to the wholeness of the rest. As a frontally open shrine and sensible navel, the cavity seems to be the charging point of the serpentine, organic shape that starts out to both sides and spreads soft reassurance. It enables the inhabitants to keep order, which is reassuring after all.

The enormous storage space provided by the shelving system is indeed able to keep both every knick-knack and all the household necessities. Behind vertical and horizontal veneers, recessed grips and clearances we can find pure practicability, including all the electronic and digital devices that we really don't wish to see out in the open anymore, but still need in an urban household to function in a halfway bearable and luxurious way.

Finally, the simple trinity of pink, white and brown opposes this trend of sophisticated randomness in terms of mixing design styles. It offers a concept: this glossy pink Wohnmaschine (referencing Le Corbusier's Unité d'habitation) as a geometrical determinant, accompanied by its little satellite, the white stripe and graph. This graph impulsively climbs up at a right angle and disappears like a digital worm above the doorframe casing behind the cupboard. At the far end of the scuncheon angle it suddenly shoots down vertically, only to stop nearly at the bottom and go horizontally from there, functioning as a so-called scuff rail that follows the space at the speed of light. The little graph as a counterpart to the long one wanders through the rooms like a gift ribbon. It seems to secure the area and hold it together, mysteriously and sweetly, just like its big sister, the all-encompassing pink perfection with sliding door.

Indeed, this unpretentious living concept strangely creates new synapses in its admirers. For the spoiled recipient however, it creates the greatest pleasure.

◇◇◇◇◇

Bei dieser andersartigen Wohnung geht das Gerücht, die Innenarchitekten seien anfangs gebeten worden, außer Tisch und Bett keine Möbel einzuplanen. Dass sich am Ende Sessel und Barhocker einschleichen durften, tut jener resoluten Entscheidung keinen Abbruch, der Kubatur anstelle diverser Schränke und Regale dieses metastatische, hellrosa Einbausystem geschlossener Tanks verpasst zu haben – auch auf die Gefahr hin, dass es eintönig würde.

Flächenbündig verblendet und lediglich im Küchenabschnitt mit seitlich offenen, furnierten Regalen bestückt, schmiegt es sich hermetisch elegant mittig durch den entkernten Grundriss und stellt alles ins Verhältnis zu sich selbst. Das interruptiv mit Gold ausgeschlagene Loch im System bildet die Ausnahme und den exotischen Bruch zur restlichen Geschlossenheit: Als eine Art frontal geöffneter

---

A potpourri of high-class chairs: SE 42 by Egon Eiermann, an Eames Side Chair with Dowel Base next to the rare Superleggera Chair by Gio Ponti for Cassina – a hot mix.

–

Potpourri aus Eins-a-Stühlen: der SE 42-Dreibeiner von Egon Eiermann, die Eames-Sidechair-Schale auf Dowel Base nebst Gio Pontis rarem Superleggera für Cassina – ein heißer Mix.

Schrein und empfänglicher Nabel scheint sich hierdurch das nach beiden Seiten schlängende Gebilde einatmend mit abstrakter Energie aufzuladen und ausatmend sanfte Beruhigung auszustrahlen. Es ermöglicht den Bewohnern, Ordnung zu halten – und das beruhigt eben.

Tatsächlich kann das Schranksystem mit seinem enormen Stauraum jeden Schnickschnack, alles Brauchbare und Nötige in sich aufnehmen; und wir finden hinter senk- und waagerechten Blenden, Klappen, vertikalen Griffmulden und engen Spaltmaßen so viel Zweckmäßigkeit versteckt, einschließlich sämtlicher elektronischer und digitaler Geräte (die man bitteschön lange schon nicht mehr sehen möchte, die ein urbaner Haushalt aber dringend benötigt, um halbwegs luxuriös und erträglich zu funktionieren).

Die simple Dreieinigkeit aus Rosa, Weiß und Braun setzt der Mode anspruchsvoller Beliebigkeit im Design-Stilmix endlich ein authentisches und beherztes, ein selbstbewusstes Konzept entgegen, nämlich die glossy rosa Wohnmaschine als geometrische Determinante, begleitet von ihrem kleinen Satelliten, dem weißen Streifen und Graphen, der impulsiv rechtwinklig wandert, digitalwurmartig als Türrahmenblende in der Horizontalität überm Schrank verschwindet und diesseitigen Endes am linken Laibungswinkel schlagartig senkrecht nach unten schießt, um knapp über Nullniveau horizontal, als sogenannte Scheuerleiste, den verwinkelten Fluchten des Raumes in Lichtgeschwindigkeit zu folgen. Der kleine Graph zieht sich als Pendant wie ein akkurates Geschenkband durch die Wohnung und scheint deren Kubatur ebenso rätselhaft und lieblich zusammenzuhalten und zu sichern wie seine die Wände umgürtende und alles in sich aufnehmende große Schwester, das vollendet eingegossene Lebenshilfemöbel mit Schiebetür.

Fürwahr, dieses unprätentiöse Wohnkonzept bildet bei Liebhabern seltsam neue Synapsen – dem verwöhnten Rezipienten vom Fach allerdings bereitet es das größte Vergnügen.

COMPOSITIONS OF CERAMIC AND STONE

———◇◇◇◇◇◇◇———

THE STALINALLEE, LATER KARL-MARX-ALLEE: SOCIALIST POMP BOULEVARD AND CULTURAL HERITAGE. HERE, PLAYFULNESS AND AUSTERITY UNITE – *DIE STALINALLEE, SPÄTER KARL-MARX-ALLEE: SOZIALISTISCHE PRACHTMA-GISTRALE UND KULTURERBE. HIER FEIERN VERSPIELTHEIT UND STRENGE HOCHZEIT*

PHOTOS: HANS-GEORG ESCH

Facade at Strausberger Platz: Built in 1952-58, the two kilometers long street with seven to nine story residential and office buildings starts here and stops at Frankfurter Tor.

—

Fassade am Strausberger Platz: Erbaut 1952-58, beginnt hier ein zwei Kilometer langer Straßenzug mit sieben- bis neungeschossigen Wohn- und Geschäftsblöcken bis hin zum Frankfurter Tor.

Arcades covered with travertine facing the street, Meissen ceramic tiles clad the upper floors. The stone cast relief of the Kino International, built in 1961-64 on the second, more modern part of the street leading to Alexanderplatz.

—

Straßenseitige Arkaden mit Travertinverblendung, das Ziegelwerk der Obergeschosse ist mit Keramik aus Meissen verkleidet. Steingussrelief am 1961-64 errichteten Kino International im zweiten, moderneren Teil der Straße Richtung Alexanderplatz.

Starting in the 18th century, ancient classical architecture has been imitated in plaster on Berlin's buildings. All the more impressive is the construction work here, on the stone columns and friezes, especially considering the circumstances during the post-war years.

—

Bereits im 18. Jahrhundert wurde an Berlins Häusern die Antike in Gips nachgeahmt. Umso höher ist die Bauleistung hier zu bewerten, an steinernen Säulen und Friesen – zumal unter schwierigsten Nachkriegsbedingungen.

Spacious and imposingly inviting public spaces are a continuous characteristic and a sign for an open and confident society.

—

Großzügige und repräsentativ-einladende öffentliche Häuserbereiche als durchgehendes Charakteristikum und Zeichen einer offenen und selbstbewussten Gesellschaft.

The exterior wall's mosaic "From the Lives of the Peoples of the Soviet Union" created in 1959 by Bert Heller at the Café Moskau and an entrance door from the first construction period illustrate contrasting diversity.

—

Das von Bert Heller im Jahr 1959 geschaffene Wandmosaik „Aus dem Leben der Völker der Sowjetunion" am Café Moskau und eine Hauseingangstür aus der ersten Bauphase verdeutlichen die kontrastreiche Vielfalt.

In the years of the apartments' completion, their fittings and amenities were way above average: long-distance heating, hot water supply, tiled bathroom, built-in kitchen, intercom and telephone connection, elevator and garbage chute.

—

Ausstattung und Komfort der Wohnungen lagen bei deren Fertigstellung weit über Durchschnitt: Fernheizung, Warmwasserversorgung, gefliestes Bad, Einbauküche, Gegensprechanlage und Telefonanschluss, Fahrstuhl und Etagen-Müllschlucker.

"Art in architecture" in the lobby of the Henselmann Tower. A mosaic by Bert Heller from 1953 that illustrates old Berlin Schlager music and adaptively embodies the "state parlor of socialism".

—

Kunst am Bau im Foyer des Henselmann-Turms: Mosaik von Bert Heller von 1953, das Altberliner Schlager illustriert und adaptiv die „Gute Stube des Sozialismus" verkörpert.

85

Elegance and order, classic principles in functional forms with politically decreed decor additions, created out of the poverty of the young republic: miracle economy instead of "Wirtschaftswunder" (economic miracle).

—

Eleganz und Ordnung, klassische Prinzipien in sachlichen Formen mit politisch abgeforderten Dekorbeigaben, aus der Armut der jungen Republik realisiert: Wunderwirtschaft statt Wirtschaftswunder.

THE MIRACLE OF FINE DESIGN PROSPERING IN SHORTAGE

IT WOULD BE EXTREMELY RUDE TO DELIVER RUBBISH TO THE CONSCIENTIOUS WORKERS INSTEAD OF HIGH-QUALITY FURNITURE, DECLARED MART STAM, DIRECTOR OF THE BERLIN KUNSTHOCHSCHULE, IN 1950 – *ES WÄRE HÖCHST UNANSTÄNDIG, DEN IN IHREN BETRIEBEN GEWISSENHAFT ARBEITENDEN SCHUND ANSTELLE HOCHWERTIG PRODUZIERTER MÖBEL ANZUBIETEN, FAND MART STAM, DIREKTOR DER BERLINER KUNSTHOCHSCHULE, 1950*

PHOTOS: RINGO PAULUSCH

The **HELLERAU PLYWOOD CHAIR 50642** by Erich Menzel, steam pressed from 29 wood layers since 1950, is high-quality, sturdy and screwless. The telephone "W58" was designed in 1958 at the Kunsthochschule Berlin-Weißensee and actually went into commercial production. — *Der Hellerauer Schichtholzstuhl „50642", von Erich Menzel, ab 1950 aus 29 Holzlagen dampfgepresst, ist hochwertig, stabil und vollkommen schraubenlos. Das Telefon „W58", 1958 an der Kunsthochschule Berlin-Weißensee gestaltet, ist tatsächlich in Großserie gegangen.*

The height-adjustable **FLOOR LAMP TYPE 8428 KONTRAST** from 1961 by the industrial designer Lutz Rudolph and the **HELLERAU DESK** of the series type 602, a design of the Bauhaus student Franz Ehrlich, form a worthy setting for the small-series model of the Tatra with a cyclop's eye for a headlight. — *Die höhenverstellbare Stehleuchte „Typ 8428 Kontrast" des Industriedesigners Lutz Rudolph von 1961 und der Schreibtisch der Hellerau-Typenserie „602", nach Entwurf des Bauhaus-Schülers Franz Ehrlich, geben ein würdiges Setting für das Modell des Tatra mit dem Zyklopenauge als Frontscheinwerfer.*

The **ELEGANT SWINGER** with strip steel base was produced mainly for public spaces and can sometimes still be found at flea markets. A very solid, modular chair from the 1960s that is quite comfortable due to a kink in the backrest. — *Eleganter Swinger mit Bandstahl-Gestell, wurde vor allem für öffentliche Räume produziert und ist auf Flohmärkten manchmal noch zu finden. Ein sehr robuster modularer Sessel aus den Sechzigern, der durch den Knick in der Rückenlehne besonders bequem ist.*

The **RATTAN CHAIRS** with black steel base from the program of the Eisu KG Themar were produced around 1958 for terraces and small spaces and are held in high esteem by design lovers. The oil painting by R. Witte from 1956 shows the International Workers' Day march on May 1st at the then-Stalinallee. — *Die Rattanstühle mit schwarzem Stahlgestell aus dem Programm der Eisu KG Themar, um 1958 für Terrassen und kleine Räume gebaut, genießen bei Designliebhabern mittlerweile hohes Ansehen. Das Ölgemälde von R. Witte 1956 zeigt die Kundgebung zum 1. Mai auf der damaligen Stalinallee.*

This foldable **OUTDOOR LOUNGE CHAIR** was called "Senftenberg Ei" in the 70s. Indeed, these egg-shaped chairs were "laid" in a Brandenburg factory close to Senftenberg and sold in many different colors. Today they sell worldwide at high prices. — *"Senftenberger Ei" nannte man in den Siebzigern diese klappbaren Sessel für den Außengebrauch. Tatsächlich wurden die Sitz-Eier in einem Brandenburger Betrieb bei Senftenberg „gelegt" und in vielen Farben verkauft. Heute werden sie international hochpreisig gehandelt.*

SPUTNIK LAMP by VEB Leuchtenbau, ca. 1970. Fancifully designed shapes of molded glass arranged in the form of a star around a middle ball to which they are connected by tubes. Back then, no one would have guessed that this model was to become iconic. — *Sputnik-Lampe, VEB Leuchtenbau, um 1970. Hier wurden an sternförmig um eine Mittelkugel angeordnete Rohre fantasievoll gestaltete Pressglaskörper befestigt. Damals ahnte keiner, dass dieses Modell in der Sammlerszene Kultstatus erlangen würde.*

ARMCHAIR MODEL 52693 by the former Bauhaus student Selman Selmanagić, designed in 1957 for the German Hellerau Workshops. The stylish plywood chair is lightweight while at the same time sturdy; high seating comfort at low material usage. — *Armlehnstuhl-Modell „52693", vom ehemaligen Bauhäusler Selman Selmanagić 1957 für die Deutschen Werkstätten Hellerau entworfen. Der Schichtholzsessel ist formschön, leicht und zugleich extrem stabil; höchster Sitzkomfort bei geringem Materialeinsatz.*

The 60s dispense with heavy furniture: **FRAGILE UPHOLSTERY** is the predecessor of the shell chair and shows a surprisingly dynamic design. They fit right into the narrow newly built flats. Colorful ceramics replace pompous porcelain and knick-knacks. — *Die 60er-Jahre räumen mit schwerem Mobiliar auf: Fragile Polstermöbel als Vorläufer der Sitzschale überraschen mit schwungvollem Design und passen gut in die engen Neubauwohnungen. Farbenfreudige Keramik löst Prunkporzellan und Nippes ab.*

In the 70s the chemical program of the GDR planned economy gathers speed. With Soviet petroleum, PUR polyurethane furniture are produced, like the so-called **KANGAROO CHAIR**, a popular all-weather outdoor furniture. — *In den Siebzigern nimmt das Chemieprogramm der DDR-Planwirtschaft Fahrt auf. Aus sowjetischem Erdöl werden auch PUR-Möbel aus Polyurethan produziert, unter anderem der sogenannte Känguru-Stuhl, ein populäres wetterfestes Gartenmöbel.*

THE BARCELONA CHAIR OF THE GDR has a better suspension than its popular role model and is more rare. The cantilever chair was designed in 1964 by Rudolph Horn, a designer from Leipzig, and produced in a small series by Röhl in Potsdam. Next to it, the small floor lamp from the former "Palast der Republik"/Berlin. — *Der DDR-Barcelona-Chair federt besser als sein berühmtes Vorbild und ist auch rarer. In kleinen Mengen wurde der vom Leipziger Designer Rudolf Horn 1964 entworfene Freischwinger von der Firma Röhl in Potsdam gefertigt. Daneben die halbhohe Stehlampe aus dem einstigen Palast der Republik/Berlin.*

The **GELENKA RELAX CHAIRS** with carrying handle, designed by Erich Diekmann in 1930, were produced in Thuringia in the 50s. The framed photograph shows: The flag carrier of the GDR was called Lufthansa as well, which posed a hefty trademark problem, so the Interflug, founded in 1958, took over. — *Die Gelenka-Relax-Sessel mit Tragegriff, Entwurf Erich Diekmann 1930, wurden in den 50er-Jahren in Thüringen hergestellt. Das gerahmte Foto verrät: Die Linienfluggesellschaft der DDR hieß — markenrechtlich hochproblematisch — ebenfalls Lufthansa, bevor die 1958 gegründete Interflug übernahm.*

A **WATERSKI** for the beach boys of the Brandenburg lakes. Germina, a combine for sports gear, engaged various manufacturers, intermittently producing this luxurious summer item, Model-S de Lux. In the background a tripod lamp with raffia shade, an early product from the Hellerau workshops. — *Ein Wasserski für die Beachboys der Brandenburger Seen. Als Kombinat für Sportausrüstung ließ Germina durch viele Hersteller produzieren, kurz auch diesen Sommer-Luxusartikel als „Modell-S de Lux". Im Hintergrund eine Tripod-Leuchte mit Bastschirm als frühes Produkt aus Hellerau.*

Goose and cube are therapeutic toys from the workshops of **RENATE MÜLLER** in Sonneberg. Produced since 1967, these objects now reach top prices at international auctions. No other toy is stuffed as hard and hence it cannot be outsourced. — *Gans und Würfel, in der Sonneberger Werkstatt von Renate Müller als therapeutische Spielfiguren seit 1967 gefertigt, erzielen heute auf internationalen Auktionen Höchstpreise. Kein Spielzeug ist so hart gestopft wie diese, daher nicht extern reproduzierbar.*

The **PUSTEBLUME** (dandelion) produced by VEB Kristallleuchte Ebersbach was a popular ornament in GDR interiors; unfortunately the lamps were very rare since most samples were bound for export. The USSR was by far the biggest customer of East German lamp production. — *Die Pusteblume, von VEB Kristalleuchte Ebersbach produziert, war ein beliebtes Schmuckstück in DDR-Wohnstuben; nur leider selten zu haben, denn die meisten Exemplare waren für den Export bestimmt. Die UdSSR war der mit Abstand größte Kunde der ostdeutschen Lampenproduktion.*

STACKING CHAIRS of this kind were produced in the GDR for cultural institutions, universities, conference halls and auditories. But they were practical for the home as well when the living room was turned into a dance floor at night. — *Stapelstühle wie dieser wurden in der DDR für Kultureinrichtungen, Hochschulen, Konferenz- und Vortragssäle produziert. Aber auch für das Zuhause waren sie praktisch, wenn das Wohnzimmer abends zum Tanzboden umfunktioniert wurde.*

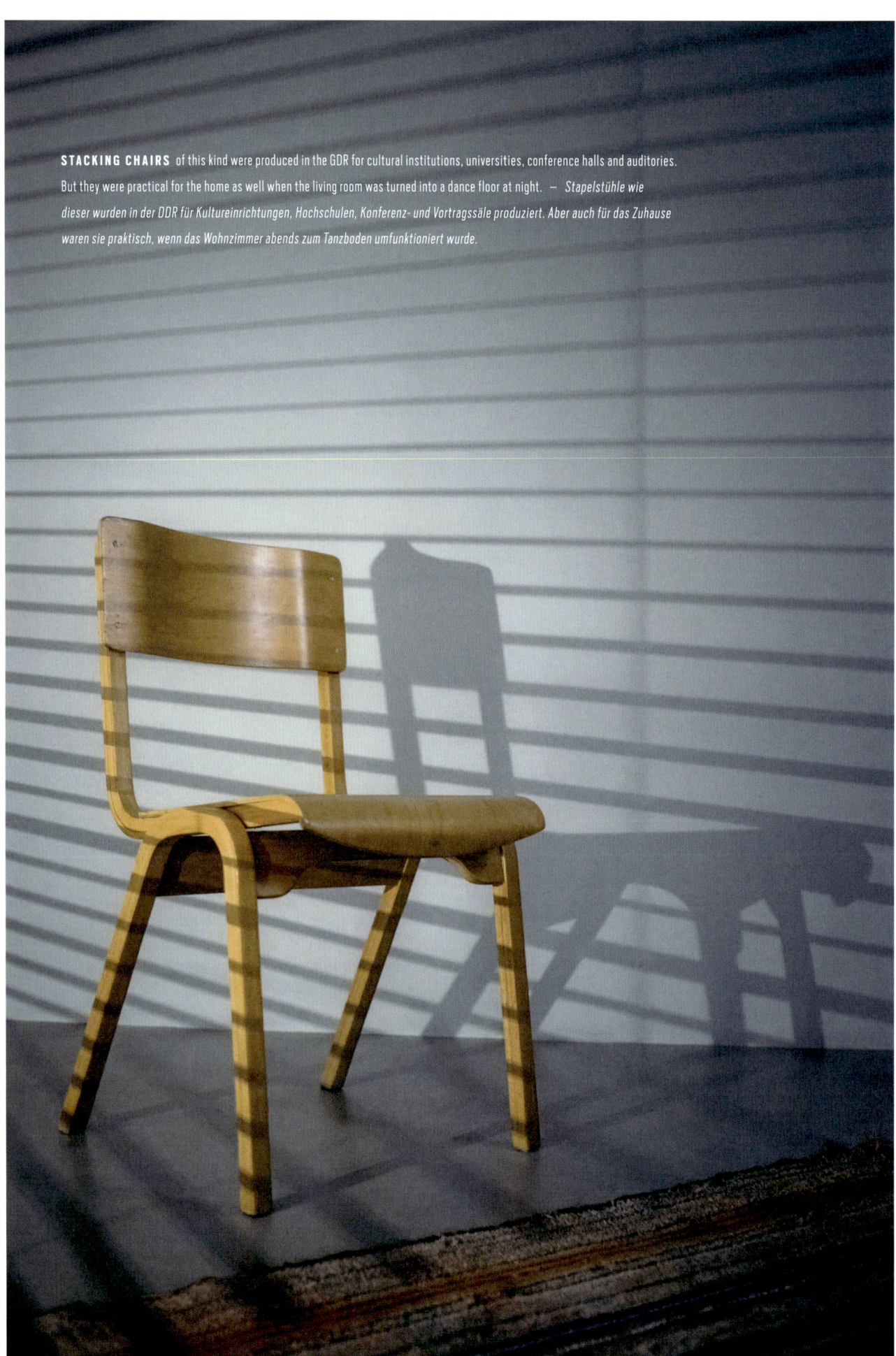

Comfortable and colorful furniture was popular in the Eastern block, too. Organic **MODULAR CHAIRS** in the style of Panton with stretch covers gather in front of the red portable TV and radio "Combi-Vision" by RTF which unfortunately broadcasted programs in black and white only. — *Auch im Ostblock liebte man es bequem und bunt, produzierte organische, an Panton angelehnte Modulsessel mit Stretchbezug. Der rote tragbare TV- und Rundfunkempfänger „Combi-Vision" von RFT strahlte das Fernsehprogramm allerdings in Schwarz-Weiß aus.*

THE RUNAWAY OF LENINPLATZ

A CURVED "PLATTENBAU" WITH PLAIN LAYOUT AND RUNNING WATER (HOT AND COLD) — *EIN KURVIGER PLATTENBAU MIT KLAREM GRUNDRISS UND FLIESSENDEM WASSER (WARM UND KALT)*

PHOTOS: JENS BÖSENBERG

Sitting in the Dieter Rams Chair "620" under Staff wall lamps you can pick your read from the shelving system on the wall. The reed green walls are a reference to their period, the original sockets and light switches have been left in their traditional positions.

—

Im Sessel „620" von Dieter Rams unter dem Staff-Leuchtentrio bedient man sich aus dem System-Regal mit Lesestoff. Die schilfgrünen Wände sind Referenz an die Bauzeit, die Steckdosen und Lichtschalter in alter Norm und Position belassen.

The circular stairs are a room object themselves and link the living area to the work space. The elevation on the door frame stems from the casing's components which have been produced with several air locks.

—

Die Wendeltreppe als Objekt im Raum verbindet Wohn- mit Arbeitsbereich. Das Profil der Türrahmung ist der Schalung aus der Produktion jener mit zahlreichen Lufteinschlüssen produzierten Bauelemente geschuldet und mutet freigelegt an wie in einem antiken Tempel.

The Egon Eiermann "E10" Chair for Heinrich Murmann on the right side and the adjacent Rams chairs and footrest pleasantly fill the sunlit room. On the walls we see an artwork by the owner.

—

Rechts ein „E10"-Korbsessel, entworfen von Egon Eiermann für Heinrich Murmann, neben den Rams-Sitzen mit Ottomane, die den lichtdurchfluteten Raum angenehm locker füllen. An der Wand eine Arbeit des Bewohners.

In front of the Eiermann table cantilever chairs from Thonet, behind them a highboard made in GDR. This arrangement is an elegant composition of Eastern and Western production.
—
Thonetschwinger am Eiermann-Tisch und das Highboard aus DDR-Herstellung dahinter zeugen in ihrer Anordnung von einer gelungenen Synthese aus Ost- und Westproduktion.

A concrete wall like the surface of a new planet with small craters is the perfect background for the bed and Thonet furniture – a well-dosed reduction. Shades of green dominate the residential studio and are even found in the safari chairs with a slight grey touch. The wall colours and Kelim carpet are perfectly matched.

—

Wie die Oberfläche eines neuen Planeten mit kleinen Kratern bildet die Betonwand Hintergrund für Bett und Thonet-Möbel – eine gelungene Reduktion. Grüntöne bestimmen die Atelierwohnung auffällig, auch in den Safari-Chairs findet sich eine gräuliche Variante; die Wandfarben sind ideal auf den Kelim abgestimmt.

Not far from Strausberger Platz we find another architecturally important ensemble with an apartment that is an excellent example of Plattenbau architecture. Hermann Henselmann, an icon of GDR architecture, built "castles for the working class" and set new standards in the late 1960s. The so-called "S-Block" and "U-Block", the initials of the Soviet Union, popularly known as "Snake" and "Boomerang", form the first building complex of its kind in East German history that is not rectangular but shaped in an atypical radial form. This was achieved by integrating trapezoidal rooms between the straight segments. Six maisonette apartments were built on the tenth and eleventh floor, each encompassing 118 sqm.

The square formerly known as Leninplatz used to have a Lenin monument at its center, which was made of red Ukrainian Kapustino granite. The 19 m high statue once gloriously looked towards the city center, but after the end of the GDR in 1989, it merely represented a failed utopia. In 1991, first the statue's head was removed, months before tearing down the entire monument. In the meantime, the headless monument served as a ridiculous symbol of an absurd demonstration of power. Stefan Heym, author, renegade and later 'Alterspräsident' (Father of the House) of the German Parliament even suggested to just leave the torso in place and merely renew the head according to the respective future leaders.

The maisonette apartment presented in this chapter witnessed those occurrences from the top of the opposing U-Block. It was designed as a residential studio. Its upper floor, a cube in the style of Mies van der Rohe, is set on top of the building and offers a light-flooded workspace. In 2000 a new resident settled in, an artist from Western Germany who still remembers the atmosphere after removing remaining fixtures, floor coverings and wall paper: "The apartment seemed to breathe again. Since then the concrete walls are bare, that old smell is gone and the apartment shines sky-high above the city. Up here even the traffic of the now-called 'Platz der Vereinten Nationen' is merely a slight humming noise." This would have pleased the architect.

◇◇◇◇◇

Unweit des Strausberger Platzes liegt ein weiteres Ensemble von architektonischer Bedeutung, dessen attraktivstes Apartment als Beispiel für Plattenbau ins Portfolio gehört. Hermann Henselmann, Ikone der DDR-Architektur und Erbauer von „Wohnpalästen für Arbeiter", konnte hier Ende der 60er-Jahre erneut Maßstäbe setzen. Denn in den sogenannten Blöcken S und U – was für Sowjet-Union steht, im Volksmund „Schlange" und „Bumerang" – findet sich erstmals die Auflösung der rechtwinkligen Form ins Radiale, indem trapezförmige Keile zwischen die Segmente gesetzt wurden: ein Novum in der ostdeutschen Baugeschichte. Ganz oben im zehnten und elften Stock entstanden sechs je 118 Quadratmeter große Maisonetten – zu DDR-Zeiten ausnahmslos regimetreuen Künstlern vorbehalten –, von denen wir eine hier vorstellen möchten.

Früher hieß die Adresse Leninplatz, ein 19 Meter hohes Lenindenkmal aus ukrainischem Kapustino-Granit blickte von der Nordseite des Platzes glorreich Richtung Stadtmitte, wirkte nach dem Ende der DDR 1989 allerdings nur noch wie das monströse Abbild einer gescheiterten Utopie. Ende 1991 wurde zunächst Lenins

Kopf entfernt, erst Monate später der Rest abgebaut – einstweilen stand der kopflose Mann als lächerliches Symbol unverständlicher Machtdemonstration da. Stefan Heym, Schriftsteller, Renegat und späterer Alterspräsident im deutschen Bundestag, erklärte hierzu, man könne den Torso ja stehenlassen und zukünftig nur den Kopf des „jeweilig Herrschenden" draufsetzen.

Unsere Maisonette im U-Block gegenüber hat dies alles von oben gesehen. Als Wohnatelier konzipiert, bildet dessen zweite Etage einen Würfel auf dem Dach des Gebäudes, der an Mies van der Rohe erinnert und lichtdurchflutet als Kreativbereich dient. 2000 zog ein neuer Mieter ein, Künstler aus dem Westen, der nach der Beseitigung verbliebener Einbauten, Auslegeware und Tapeten erzählt: „Die Wohnung schien aufzuatmen. Die Betonwände liegen seitdem frei, der Muff ist beseitigt und das Apartment strahlt in luftiger Höhe über der Stadt, so weit oben, dass man den Verkehr am neugetauften Platz der Vereinten Nationen nur noch als leises Surren wahrnimmt." Dem Erbauer hätte es gefallen.

High above the roofs of Berlin you may free your mind. A roof garden with all-season plants convey the feeling of having one's own "outdoors" inside the city.

—

Über den Dächern Berlins lässt es sich anders denken. Ganzjährige Pflanzen im Dachgarten garantieren das Gefühl, mitten in der Stadt ein eigenes „Draußen" zu haben.

Chipped tiles form a new relief that is part of a blocky wall design with a selfmade plywood rack.
—
Abgeschlagene Fliesen bilden ein neues Relief als Teilabschnitt einer blockartigen Wandgestaltung mit selbst kreiertem Wandregal aus Schichtholz.

ART, AURA, ANARCHY...

WHEN FOUR WALLS CREATE A SURREAL LAB, CULTIVATED BY INTERNAL CHAOS — *WENN VIER WÄNDE EIN SURREALES LABOR BILDEN, VOM INNEREN CHAOS KULTIVIERT*

PHOTOS: MARTIN MAI

Old school drawing board, copier on wheels, brand tin signs on the walls as ornaments. The structured room tells a tale of mystery and the value of significance.

—

Old-school-Zeichenbrett, Kopierer auf Rollen, Verpackungsreliefs als Wandornamente. Der Strukturraum erzählt von Mystik und Nutzen der Signifikanzen.

The insurrection of signs, objects, designs. All items inspire individually and once again exponentially as a mysterious mixture.

—

Aufstand der Zeichen, Objekte, Modelle. Alles Einzelne inspiriert, in Summe und rätselhafter Vermischung noch einmal exponentiell.

Theatrical settings in an illuminated model. In the beginning is the idea, today you can watch the master cook his artistic recipes of set decoration.

—

Theatrale Settings im ausgeleuchteten Modell. Am Anfang steht die Idee, und heute kann man den Meister beim Kochen zusehen.

Who's living in this extraordinary residence? Is it a film director, an artist, a set designer or maybe a borderline patient? Ancient typewriters and other items that reference an analogue world, rather than the displaced high-tech components, suggest a sophisticated man of attitude: is he a poet? Does he create his lines among all these metallic objects, these industrial society styrofoam ornaments on the walls, all these mysterious phantoms of the imagination that refuse to make any sense?

Alien cell doors that function as room dividers, sculptural indifference in clusters evoke a secret adeptness and the knowledge of pain. The surroundings seem to have been in constant use, as if the books rearrange themselves according to urban tides, as if the paintings and photos change their positions nightly. It seems as if the spaceship-like organism, just like an abstract biosphere, permanently gives birth to something unique and new – an eerie but at the same time intoxicating chaos that seems to be inhabited by a tireless spirit. Cheekily the chaos appears to be asking the visitor whether he has arrived to disturb.

This creative space is up in the tower at Strausberger Platz, taking up 160 sqm. It is apartment and artist's studio at the same time; though not comfortable, it is still inviting. Hardly any furniture to rest but still a techno-dreamscape that both baffles and beguiles you. If you would like to watch the furniture being moved or the artist at work painting or lecturing, you just have to settle for standing or sitting down on the parquet floor. This room, bursting with personality, does not seem to care either way. Long before the fall of the Berlin Wall, the room served as refuge and safe haven for the stage man and his entourage against the GDR blueshirts. Even today, it still feels as though here one could safely hide from the cold and grey world beyond these doors.

◇◇◇◇◇

Wer wohnt in dieser extraordinären Residenz? Ist es ein Regisseur, ein Künstler, ein Bühnenbildner oder ein Borderliner? Uralte Schreibmaschinen und andere analoge Referenzen, neben Hightech-Versatz, lassen auf einen Mann des Ausdrucks in Gestus und Wort schließen: Ist es ein Poet? Finden sich seine Zeilen wieder gegossen in jene umstehenden metallischen Objekte, in den industriegesellschaftlichen Styropor-ornamenten an den Wänden, all jenen rätselhaften Phantasiegebilden, deren Sinn sich nicht verraten will?

Aus der Welt gefallene Gefängnistüren als Raum-Zeit-Teiler, skulpturale Indifferenzen im Cluster evozieren geheime Erfahrungen und Wissen um Schmerz. Alles Vorhandene wirkt wie im ständigen Gebrauch, als ob sich die Bücher im urbanen Gezeitenrhythmus umstapelten, die Gemälde und Fotos nachts heimlich ihre Positionen tauschten. Und überhaupt, als ob der raumschiffartige Organismus wie eine abstrakte Biosphäre permanent Neues gebierte – ein unheimliches und doch so entzündendes Chaos, dem ein nimmermüder Geist innezuwohnen scheint, observiert den Besucher und scheint diesen keck zu fragen, ob er stören will.

Im Turm am Strausberger Platz auf 160 Quadratmetern liegt dieser Kreativraum, Wohnung und Atelier zugleich. Nicht komfortabel und doch einladend, kaum Ruhemöbel und doch Techno-Traum-Landschaft, die bremst und betört. Dann muss man sich halt stehenderweise einrichten oder einen Sitzplatz auf dem

Parkett suchen, um beim Möbelrücken zuzusehen oder dem Hausherrn beim Zeichnen, beim Dozieren. Diesem vor Individualität strotzenden Raum scheint das alles völlig egal zu sein; bereits vor der Wende war er dem Theatermann und seiner Entourage Refugium und Rückzugsort vor den Blauhemden der DDR. Das merkt man ihm heute noch an, und nach einer Weile des Hierseins fühlt man sich seltsam versteckt und geborgen vor der kalten grauen Welt jenseits der Türen.

The pale built-in cabinet is the last relic of bygone Stalinist kitchen designs. It bravely defies the red boxing gloves that dangle so provocatively cheerful from the ceiling.

—

Der blasse Einbauschrank als letztes Relikt stalinistischer Küchenbauweise trotzt den roten Boxhandschuhen, die herausfordernd poppig von der Decke baumeln.

The iconography of transition is illustrated by the cell door with hatch. It separates the inside world from the outside.
—
Ikonografie des Übergangs, illustriert durch die Zellentür mit Durchreiche, die das Innen vom Außen trennt.

NIGHT WALK ALONG THE AVENUE

---◇◇◇◇◇◇◇◇◇---

BY NIGHT THE "KU'DAMM OF THE EAST" SHINES AT PROMINENT POINTS. AN INKLING OF THE UPCOMING BOOM SETS IN – *BEI NACHT ERSTRAHLT DER „KU'DAMM DES OSTENS" AN MARKANTEN STELLEN. MAN GLAUBT DEN BEVORSTEHENDEN BOOM ZU ERAHNEN*

PHOTOS: RINGO PAULUSCH

The **KOSMOS CINEMA** opened in 1962 as the GDR's biggest movie theater with 1,001 seats. It is a prestressed concrete construction comparable to the Congress Hall in West Berlin. The high elliptical main building and cinema hall is embedded in a surrounding single-floor rectangle containing a glazed entrance hall. — Das „Kosmos"-Kino, eröffnet 1962 als größtes Kino der DDR mit 1.001 Sitzplätzen, ist eine Spannbetonkonstruktion, vergleichbar mit der Westberliner Kongresshalle. Ein hoher elliptischer Bau, Hauptgebäude und Kinosaal, steckt in einem eingeschossigen Rechteck, das als Umgrenzung und Vorbau mit verglaster Eingangshalle dient.

The cinema **KINO INTERNATIONAL** is a three-story building of reinforced concrete framework veneered with light sandstone. Its three windowless lateral surfaces show a colorful sculptural relief with the title "Of the Lives of Today's People". To the front side the second floor, cantilevering 9 m above the ground floor and encompassing 35 m width, houses a bar with an immense window front. The cinema hall is designed for 600 people and equipped with an 18 m large screen and sophisticated acoustics that make screenings truly unique events. — *Das „Kino International", eröffnet 1963, ist ein dreigeschossiger Stahlbetonskelettbau, der mit hellem Sandstein verkleidet wurde. Die drei fensterlosen Seitenflächen ziert ein bewegtes Bildhauerrelief mit dem Titel „Aus dem Leben heutiger Menschen"; nach vorne bildet das neun Meter übers Erdgeschoss kragende und 35 Meter breite Obergeschoss als Bar eine riesige Fensterfront. Der für über 600 Menschen konzipierte Kinosaal hat eine großzügige, fast 18 Meter breite Leinwand und macht Filmrezeptionen einzigartig, nicht zuletzt wegen seiner ausgeklügelten Akustik.*

BRIEFMARKEN an upscale restaurant with an Italian touch in a former stamp shop. It offers not only haute cuisine but also select wines and desserts. — *Briefmarkenweine; im alten Briefmarkengeschäft befindet sich ein edles Speisenrestaurant mit italienischem Einschlag. Hier gibt es neben gehobener Küche auch erlesene Weine und Desserts.*

BAR BABETTE once a beauty parlor for the modern East-German woman with manicure and pedicure booths in the mezzanine. Furs from the vast Soviet tundra were intermittently sold on the main floor of the glass building. Today it's a place where cocktails are shaken and stirred. — *„Bar Babette", ehemals Kosmetiksalon für die moderne Frau des Ostens mit Maniküre- und Pedikürekabinen im Mezzanin. Der gläserne Bau bot im Erdgeschoss zeitweise Pelze aus den Weiten der sowjetischen Tundra. Heute werden hier Cocktails geschüttelt und gerührt.*

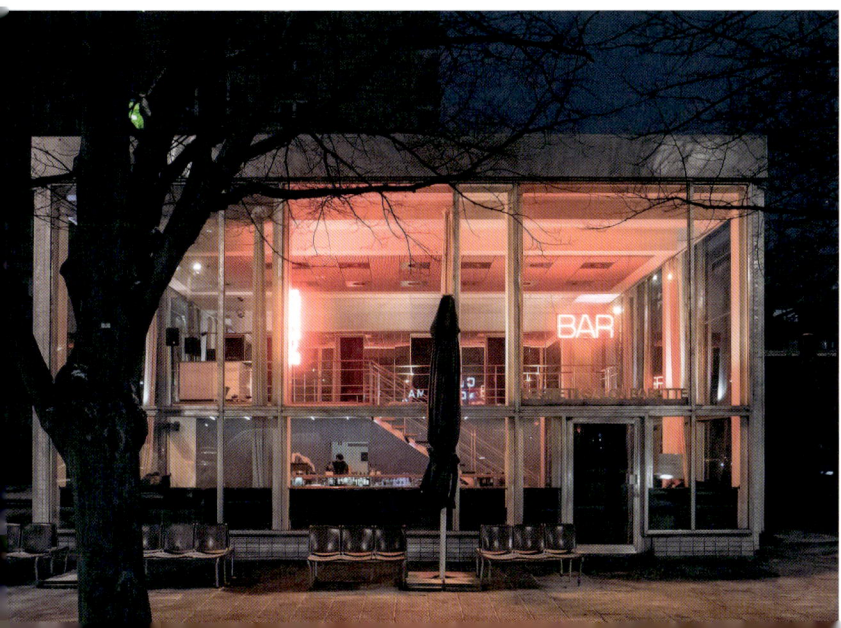

The **CAFÉ SIBYLLE** opened in 1962 as a milk bar, named after the women's magazine, the East-German version of "Vogue". The magazine deliberately left out advice columns to promote fashion as a form of art, manifested in various photo series by prominent artists. Since 2002 the café has also been a venue for exhibitions and readings. – Das „Café Sibylle", eröffnet 1962 als Milchtrinkhalle, wurde nach der gleichnamigen Frauenzeitschrift benannt, jener Ost-„Vogue", die bewusst auf Ratgeberteile verzichtete, um die Mode als Kunstform in den Vordergrund zu stellen, was sich in den Fotostrecken von namhaften Künstlern manifestierte. Seit 2002 finden hier auch Ausstellungen und Lesungen statt.

The **COMPUTERSPIELEMUSEUM** opened in 2011 in the former "Café Warschau", which was inaugurated on May 1st 1953, spread out over two floors linked by a flight of stairs. It used to be a restaurant of different nationalities with polish culinary art. Today the museum's permanent exhibition shows one of the biggest collections of entertainment software and hardware in Europe. – Das Computerspielemuseum eröffnete 2011 im ehemaligen „Café Warschau", das 1953 zum 1. Mai eingeweiht wurde. Es präsentierte sich auf zwei Etagen, die durch eine Freitreppe verbunden waren, als Nationalitätenrestaurant mit polnischen Kulinaria. Heute beherbergt das Museum in der ständigen Ausstellung eine der größten Sammlungen von Entertainmentsoft- und -hardware in Europa.

Since 2008 the only thing left of the **KARL-MARX-BUCHHANDLUNG**, opened in 1953, is the landmarked logo. The space is currently being used as an archive and is waiting to be reawakened as a bookstore. — *Von der Karl-Marx-Buchhandlung, eröffnet 1953, existiert seit 2008 nur noch der denkmalgeschützte Schriftzug. Es wird derzeit als Archiv benutzt und wartet darauf, wieder als Buchhandlung wachgeküsst zu werden.*

The **CAFÉ MOSKAU** opened in 1964 as a venue and multinational restaurant. It is famous for its transparency created by the atrium design. In the 1980s darkening elements were added by order of the petty bourgeois nomenklatura, depriving the building of its modern look. But since the renovation in 2007, it once again shines in old transparency. — Das „Café Moskau", eröffnet 1964 als Nationalitätenrestaurant und Veranstaltungsort, berühmt wegen seiner gläsernen Transparenz durch die offene Atriumbauweise. In den 80er-Jahren auf Geheiß der kleinbürgerlichen Nomenklatura durch konspirativ verdunkelnde Einbauten seiner modernen Anmutung beraubt, strahlt es seit der Sanierung 2007 wieder in alter Durchsichtigkeit.

PERES PROJECTS international gallery with changing temporary exhibitions and fairs from around the world including New York and Los Angeles. — Peres Projects; Internationale Galerie mit wechselnden Ausstellungen und Messen, unter anderem in New York und Los Angeles

ORIGINAL IN BERLIN Midcentury Furniture and Accessories from East and West. Classics, rare high-quality pieces of premium origins that can be restored in the integrated carpenter's and upholsterer's workshop if needed. The right shop in the right place for a stylish interior. — Original in Berlin; Midcentury Füllhorn mit Möbeln und Accessoires aus Ost und West. Absolute Designklassiker, auch Rares von hoher Qualität und edler Herkunft wird wenn nötig sofort nach Ankauf in der integrierten Werkstatt von Tischler und Polsterer restauriert. Der richtige Shop am rechten Ort ermöglicht stilechtes Einrichten.

Unscheduled nights like this, between two meticulously planned workdays, are promising something, like the days used to when we were children, when life had not been structured yet and things just happened. Today I had a bunch of conversations with different people; among others with this somewhat older lady, a very neat and attractive historian. Tomorrow at twelve o'clock an airport taxi will be waiting for me downstairs on the boulevard for my journey back home. So I could either get up early in the morning to stroll around the neighborhood, getting to know it, and take pictures in sunlight. Or I can just put on something warm after a quick bath and sneak out into the night past my hostess - who knows what's waiting for me out there? I ponder, choose the road less pleasant and decide to sleep in tomorrow.

Upon leaving the tower I sense two lovers kissing under the arcades at Strausberger Platz. I hurry to reach the illuminated boulevard. Which direction should I take? Just let myself wander. Wow, quickly get the camera, these perspectives are gigantomaniac - superreal. According to the great Italian architect Aldo Rossi, this is Europe's last large-scale boulevard, with 90 m distance between the buildings larger than the Champs-Élysées. I remember the historian's stochastic stories on the neighborhood: 38 million bricks were recovered from the rubble and form 70% of the ensemble's structure. Around four million voluntary working hours were spent on this grand boulevard. How enthusiastically these people set to work? All because they were secretly hoping to build "palaces for the working class" that would include also their own three-bedroom apartment?

I cross over to the large green median dividing the eight-lane road to completely take in the symmetry of the prospekt. Approaching cars are honking for no reason, up on a third-floor balcony people are dancing and smoking at a noisy party. I am overcome by a feeling of happiness. Something happens above me, the sky opens and uncovers a giant full moon in accordance with my perspective on the vanishing point at the end of the boulevard. This sensation makes me want to pivot around my own axis, faster and faster, until bells are ringing.

This is where, in 1953, the workers' uprising took place. If I remember the lady's pleasant full voice correctly, it turned into a mighty riot against the Socialist Unity Party and the Soviet forces leading, in West Germany, to the creation of the "Day of German Unity" on June 17th 1954 until the political turnaround in 1989/90 to commemorate the events that took place on this famous terrain .

The workers´ uprising was caused by the bad supply situation and the inability of the mason collective to keep up with the fast-paced demands of the political leaders, that continuously extended targets and work quotas. This is what an old man tells me at the bar that I ended up at after my long walk and the many photo breaks. Beauty has once again arisen from suffering and deprivation. Enlightened storeis. By night, when life slows down, they appear out of the dark, satisfy my curiosity and make urban dreams come true - one wishes to be part of it. Here is where I want to live; I will be back.

◇◇◇◇◇◇

Eine Nacht, ungeplant zwischen zwei penibel durchgetakteten Arbeitstagen, irgendetwas verheißend, wie damals in Kindertagen, als das Leben noch keine Struktur kannte und die Dinge einfach passierten. Heute waren eine Menge Gespräche mit mehr oder weniger interessanten Menschen; auch mit dieser schon etwas älteren, sehr gepflegten und attraktiven Historikerin. Morgen wartet um zwölf Uhr unten in der Allee das Flughafentaxi zur Heimreise. Ich könnte also entweder früh aufstehen, um flanierenderweise den Kiez kennenzulernen und ihn in der Sonne abzufotografieren; oder ich kann mich nach einem kurzen Bad warm anziehen und an meiner Gastgeberin vorbei in die Nacht hinausschleichen – wer weiß, was mich da draußen erwartet. Ich wäge ab, nehme den unangenehmeren Weg und entscheide mich dafür, morgen auszuschlafen.

Beim Verlassen des Turmes erahne ich in den dunklen Arkaden am Strausberger Platz zwei Liebende, die sich küssen. Ich beeile mich, auf die Allee zu kommen ins Licht. Welche Richtung soll ich nehmen? Einfach treiben lassen. Wow, schnell die Kamera, diese Perspektiven sind gigantomanisch – superreal. Dem großen italienischen Architekten Aldo Rossi zufolge ist dies der letzte großangelegte Boulevard in Europa: Mit 90 Metern Abstand zwischen den Hausfronten ist er breiter als die Champs-Élysées.

Ich erinnere mich an die stochastischen Erzählungen der Historikerin über den Kiez: 38 Millionen Ziegelsteine wurden aus dem Schutt geborgen und bildeten 70 Prozent der Bausubstanz dieses Ensembles. Rund vier Millionen Stunden freiwilliger Arbeit wurden für den Prachtboulevard geleistet. Mit welchem Enthusiasmus sind diese Menschen ans Werk gegangen? Und dies alles nur, weil sie im Stillen hofften, in den Fassadenbauten Paläste für Arbeiter entstehen zu lassen, die insgeheim auch für sie selbst eine „Dreiraumwohnung" vorsahen?

Ich wechsle auf den begrünten, ewig breiten Mittelstreifen zwischen den vierspurigen Strecken, um die Symmetrie des gesamten Prospekts auf meine Gehirnhälften wirken zu lassen. Entgegenkommende Autos hupen grundlos, dort oben auf dem Balkon im dritten Stock tanzen rauchende Menschen, Teil einer lauten Party. Ein Glücksgefühl überkommt mich. Über mir passiert etwas, der Nachthimmel reißt auf und legt einen riesigen Vollmond frei, der den Gleichklang meiner Perspektive auf den Fluchtpunkt am Ende der Allee konzentriert, und dieser Eindruck bewirkt, dass ich mich drehen möchte, um die eigene Achse, immer schneller. Bis die Glocken läuten.

Hier fand also 1953 der Arbeiteraufstand statt, der, wenn ich die Inhalte der angenehm sonoren Historikerinnenstimme recht erinnere, zu einer mächtigen Revolte gegen die SED-Führung und die sowjetischen Machthaber ausartete und in der Bundesrepublik Deutschland durch den „Tag der deutschen Einheit" ab dem 17. Juni 1954 bis zur politischen Wende 1989/90 Würdigung und Gedenken fand – so berühmt ist das Terrain.

Der Aufstand brach aus wegen der schlechten Versorgungslage und der Überforderung der Maurerkollektive durch ständig erweiterte Planziele und Akkordvorgaben der politischen Führung, erzählt mir der alte Mann in der Bar, die ich nach einem langen Spaziergang mit vielen Fotopausen geentert habe. Also ist auch hier mal wieder alles Schöne aus Leid und Entbehrung hervorgegangen. Was für erhellende Geschichten. Bei Nacht, wenn sich das Leben verlangsamt, treten sie ins Licht, stillen meine Wissbegierde und verheißen die Erfüllung aller Großstadtträume – man möchte ein Teil davon sein. Hier will ich leben; ich komme wieder.

THE REAL BALANCE BETWEEN WORKING AND LIVING

WHEN INDIVIDUAL INTERIOR DESIGN MAKES NO DIFFERENCE BETWEEN PRIVACY AND OFFICE – *WENN INDIVIDUELLE WOHNKULTUR KEINEN UNTERSCHIED MEHR MACHT ZWISCHEN ZUHAUSE UND BÜRO*

PHOTOS: MARTIN MAI

Bright, brighter. Original Eames Side Chairs on H-Bases at Tulip Table by Saarinen. Into the overall white cuts the soft wood grain of the floor boards and the cabinet. This is as clear as it gets.
—
Hell und heller. Originale Eames-Sidechairs auf H-Bases vor dem Tuliptisch von Saarinen. Ins Weiße sticht die sanfte Holzmaserung der Dielen und des Schranks – klarer geht's nicht.

Production: Andreas Tölke

An interplay of black, white and grey tones contrasts the brown of the wooden surfaces. In between classics like the armchair LC 2 by Le Corbusier or the Lounge Chair by Charles and Ray Eames.

—

Spiel mit Schwarz-, Weiß- und Grautönen als Kontrast zur Wärme der Holzoberflächen. Dazwischen Klassiker, wie der Sessel LC 2 von Le Corbusier oder der Lounge Chair von Charles und Ray Eames.

The living area and office of an architects duo inside the Henselmann Tower unite two floors. Due to their formal similarity, the spaces form a novel interior synthesis. This is seen in the objectification of the furniture and hence of the private sphere as well as in the monochromy of the setting. Contrarily, the office space is embellished with curtains, various seatings and wall decoration creating a quite cosy atmosphere. Besides a sleeping area and a bathroom, what more does an apartment need than merely a table, chairs, shelving systems and perhaps a corner to relax in? Here these criteria are met with a through-composed simplicity. Archetypes of design receive their well-deserved aura in this puristic space with no chichi, almost as if it had always been this way.

The view from the living room over the kitchen aisle into the bathroom offers several successive levels of perception. It transports the semi-public sphere of the private area to an intimate one. A horizontal bar hanging on ropes turns out to be a very cool and hidden accessory of the playing field. The 3 m high mirrored sliding door serves as room divider and as a reflection device for a final look in the mirror before going out. These spaces are ideal for set-ups. In here unique items gain universal relevance, as if being in one of those hip galleries in Manhattan's Village. This continues seamlessly in the work space that gives relevance to every intentionally placed item, functionally arranged to create a harmonious constellation. Even those who don't appreciate reduced spaces have to admit that in this office and living arrangement, it is particularly the amount of space given to the objects that liberates the mind and inspires the imagination.

◇◇◇◇◇◇

Auf zwei Etagen verbinden sich Wohn- und Arbeitswelt eines Architektenduos im Henselmann-Turm und bilden in ihrer formalen Ähnlichkeit eine ganz neuartige Interior-Synthese: Zum einen durch Versachlichung der Privatsphäre in der mobiliaren Ausstattung und Einfarbigkeit des Settings, zum anderen durch die gemütlich-individuelle Beseelung des Bürotrakts mit Vorhängen, unterschiedlicher Bestuhlung und Wandschmuck. Was benötigt eine Wohnung neben Schlaf- und Waschbereich mehr als Tisch, Stühle, Regale und eventuell eine Ecke zum Relaxen? Diese Kriterien werden in durchkomponierter Schlichtheit erfüllt. Puristisch und ohne Chichi stehen Archetypen frei an ihrem Platz, als wäre es schon immer so gewesen, und erhalten verdiente Aura.

Der Durchblick vom Wohnzimmer über die Küchennische ins Bad bildet hintereinander geschichtete Wahrnehmungsebenen und entrückt das Halböffentliche vom Privaten hin zum Intimen. Cool sind die vordergründig sinnfreie Reckstange an Seilen als vieldeutiges Spielwiesen-Accessoire, die über drei Meter hohe verspiegelte Schiebetür als verdoppelnder Raumtrenner und Reflektionsapparatur? In diesen Räumen läßt sich inszenieren. Unikate erhalten universale Relevanz, wie in einer dieser hippen Galerien in Manhattans Village. Was sich im Bürotrakt nahtlos fortführt, der ebenfalls jedem durchdacht gesetzten Gegenstand Wirkungsraum gibt und über die funktionale Anordnung der Items harmonische Konstellationen bildet. Auch wer reduzierte Räume nicht goutiert, muss nach Besuch dieser Wohnarbeitswelt zugeben, dass gerade durch dieses Den-Dingen-Platz-Geben Raum für Fantasie und die Entwicklung freier Gedanken bleiben.

Private color schemes reappear in the office section. A consequent use of black and white right down to the desks is completed by the interplay of light and shadows in the coffering of the ceiling.

—

Private Farbwelten tauchen im Bürotrakt wieder auf. Konsequenter Einsatz von Schwarz und Weiß bis zu den Schreibtischen, komplettiert durch Licht- und Schattenspiele in der Deckenkassettierung.

Straight lines, a set of rooms, variety of material. These photographs could easily be found under the chapter "modern office" in a global almanac for interior design.
—
Gerade Linien, Zimmerfluchten, Materialvielfalt. Im Kapitel eines globalen Interior-Almanachs könnten diese Fotos klassisch für „Modernes Büro" stehen.

ZERO HOUR.
THE DEVELOPMENT
OF A STREET
THEN AND NOW

THE HISTORY OF EUROPE'S LAST GREAT BOULEVARD – *ÜBER DIE ENTSTEHUNG DES LETZTEN GROSSEN BOULEVARDS IN EUROPA*

ca. 1950 — Apartments are occupied, shops are opened; due to the bad supply situation a shopping stroll on 1950s Stalinallee means longingly window shopping along mostly empty displays. Throughout the generations the population appears in a neat, often self-tailored bearing, despite the shortage. — *Die Wohnungen sind bezogen, die Geschäfte eröffnet; Einkaufsbummel in der Stalinallee der 50er-Jahre bedeutet sehnsuchtsvolles Hineinblicken in die großen Schaufenster, deren Auslagen aufgrund der Versorgungslage selten prall gefüllt sind. Dieser Mangel hält die Bevölkerung jedoch nicht davon ab, quer durch die Generationen im gepflegten, oftmals selbst geschneiderten Habitus aufzutreten.*

1946 Frankfurter Allee, later called Stalinallee, in 1946: A wide cut through the field of rubble shows the extent of the destruction. One year earlier the "glorious Soviet army" passed through this former Reichsstraße using heavy artillery towards conquering the city center where the Reich Chancellery and Führerbunker (Leader's bunker) were located, and in the course destroying not only hideouts of last Nazi resistance movements but also the last vestiges of civil life. Now thousands of voluntary unpaid workers must select still useful construction material from the rubble. – *Die Frankfurter Allee, später Stalinallee, im Jahr 1946: Eine breite Schneise durch das Trümmerfeld offenbart das Ausmaß der Zerstörung. Ein Jahr zuvor hatte sich die „ruhmreiche sowjetische Armee" ihren Weg mit schwerer Artillerie durch genau diese ehemalige Reichsstraße zur Eroberung der Stadtmitte mit Reichskanzlei und Führerbunker gebahnt und neben den Nestern des NS-Widerstands auch die letzten Spuren von zivilem Leben zerschossen. Nun gilt es, mit tausenden freiwilligen und unbezahlten Arbeitskräften aus dem Schutt das brauchbare Baumaterial herauszulesen.*

1951/52

The model of the construction project Weberwiese shows the eight-story apartment house built in 1951/52, designed by Hermann Henselmann. It became the signature project for the Stalinallee, because it was the first design in conformity with the political system. The first design was too modern and formalistic. Thus, upon orders of the Soviets, the German architect team added Prussian classicist elements to the design within eight days, and so the designs were promptly approved. This would set the course: more Schinkel, less Bauhaus. Many details on the buildings show antique elements: Ionic or Doric columns, friezes and architrave pediments. – *Das Modell des Bauprojekts Weberwiese zeigt das 1951/52 errichtete achtgeschossige Hochhaus von Hermann Henselmann, welches als Leitbau die architektonische Handschrift für die Stalinallee vorgab, weil hier zum ersten Mal ein systemkonformer Stil erkennbar wurde. Der erste Entwurf der Allee war zu formalistisch-modern, wurde auf Anordnung der Sowjets vom deutschen Architektenteam innerhalb von acht Tagen preußisch-klassizistisch modifiziert und prompt bewilligt. Damit war die Richtung vorgegeben: mehr Schinkel, weniger Bauhaus. An vielen Stellen der Gebäude finden sich daher Zitate antiker Einzelformen, ionische oder dorische Säulen, Friese und Ziergiebel mit Architrav.*

1952   In 1952 the 2nd party conference of the SED (Socialist Unity Party of Germany) discussed the construction projects of the GDR using also this model of Stalinallee. It shows the linear layout of monolithic facade architecture like Potemkin villages, suggesting an imposing urban feeling to visitors of the central boulevard. But behind these facades large undeveloped parcels of land were hidden, evidence of the republic's shortcomings since its formation in 1949, facing an enormous wave of emigration of skilled workers and the educated middle class until the construction of the Berlin Wall in 1961. What remains is the longest architectural monument of the former GDR. —

1952 diskutierte die II. Parteikonferenz der SED die Bauvorhaben in der DDR anhand auch dieses Modells von der Stalinallee. Es veranschaulicht die spalierartige Anordnung von monolithischen Fassadenbauten als Potemkinsche Dörfer, die dem Besucher der inneren Allee zwar imponieren und das Gefühl von mächtiger Urbanität suggerieren. Dahinter allerdings erkennt man große unbebaute Brachen als Armutszeugnisse einer Republik, die seit Entstehung 1949 einem enormen Aderlass von Fachkräften und Bildungsbürgern ausgesetzt ist, bis der Mauerbau 1961 dem ein abruptes Ende setzt. Geblieben ist das längste Architekturdenkmal der ehemaligen DDR.

Hermann Henselmann surveys designs of architectural details at a Berlin sculptor's workshop. Decisions regarding style and decoration were made in a minimum of time since many foundation pits were excavated even before plannings were completed. It all had to work without any digital aids in a city where streets were ruined and supply lines were cut off. The reconstruction work during those years deserves high acclaim. — *Hermann Henselmann begutachtet in einem Berliner Bildhaueratelier Entwürfe für Architekturdetails. Innerhalb kürzester Zeit mussten viele Entscheidungen hinsichtlich Stil und Dekoration getroffen werden, denn oftmals waren die Baugruben bereits ausgehoben, bevor die Planungen abgeschlossen waren. All dies ohne digitale Hilfsmittel in einem Berlin mit kaputten Straßen und gekappten Versorgungsleitungen. Man kann die Aufbauleistung jener Jahre nicht hoch genug bewerten.*

1952

The "Cathedrals of Capital" in the United States were the model for the Soviet "Palaces of the Peoples' Power" – only that the latter had an additional layer of decorative frosting. Below left the 177 m high Municipal Building in New York, built between 1907-14; above it Moscow's foreign ministry with a height of 171 m, built during the Stalin era in 1948-53. The architecture of the early Soviet years was inspired by a building of the class enemy of all things. It became a paradigm for East Berlin. – *Die „Kathedralen des Kapitals" in den USA waren die Vorbilder für die sowjetischen „Paläste der Volksmacht" – jene allerdings mit noch einem Schuss Zuckerguss obendrauf. Unten links das 177 Meter hohe Municipal Building in New York, errichtet von 1907-14, darüber das 171 Meter hohe Außenministerium in Moskau, erbaut unter Josef Stalin von 1948-53. Die Architektur der großen sowjetischen Aufbaujahre hatte sich ausgerechnet an einem Gebäude des Klassenfeindes ein Beispiel genommen und wurde zum Vorbild für Ostberlin.*

1948-53

1952   1952, the first topping-out ceremony at Stalinallee with the party and state leaders of the "Pankow Regime" on the podium. To this day, the get-up-and-go-spirit of the flagged setting during the first construction phase between Strausberger Platz and Frankfurter Tor conveys the pride of the young republic. The photo also shows the bold scaffolding constructions reaching way above the eaves of the buildings which today would certainly not pass a building inspection. — *1952 das erste Richtfest in der Stalinallee mit der Partei- und Staatsführung des „Pankower Regimes" auf dem Podium. Die Baut-Auf-Stimmung im beflaggten Umfeld des ersten Bauabschnitts zwischen Strausberger Platz und Frankfurter Tor vermittelt noch heute den Stolz der jungen Republik. Das Foto zeigt auch die verwegenen Gerüstkonstruktionen bis weit über die Fassadenenden, die heute keiner baupolizeilichen Prüfung standhalten würden.*

ca. 1957   View through the sandstone arcades across Strausberger Platz in the late 1950s onto the street theater. The completed buildings towards Frankfurter Tor shine brightly. The brickwork behind the cladded facade was mostly recovered from the debris of the old Frankfurter Allee and put into construction by taskwork. In the left corner of the photo we see the pre-WWII buildings that used to be behind the ensemble. — *Blick durch die Sandsteinarkaden über den Strausberger Platz Ende der 50er-Jahre auf das Straßentheater. Hell erstrahlen die fertiggestellten Häuser Richtung Frankfurter Tor. Das Ziegelwerk hinter den verkleideten Fassaden wurde größtenteils aus den Trümmern der alten Frankfurter Allee gewonnen und im Akkord verbaut. Hinter dem Ensemble stehen damals noch Altbauten, was am linken Bildrand gut zu erkennen ist.*

1953

Among the first tenants were many outstanding workers of the construction phase of Stalinallee. In the background, the towers at Strausberger Platz under construction, in the front the mason brigade, not properly dressed for the winter weather, who wanted to attend the event. The general pride was manifested ostentatiously, it was all political. Even moving into one's own newly built full comfort flat became a propagandistic act. — *Unter den ersten Mietern waren auch viele „Bestarbeiter" der Baustelle Stalinallee. Im Hintergrund die noch im Bau befindlichen Türme des Strausberger Platzes, vorne im Bild die fürs winterliche Wetter sehr spärlich bekleideten Maurerbrigaden, die beim Ereignis dabei sein wollen. Der allgemeine Stolz inszenierte sich demonstrativ, alles war politisch, selbst der private Umzug ins neue Heim mit Vollkomfort wurde zum propagandistischen Akt.*

ca. 1955   A smoking couple in their thoroughly designed living room. It seems as though he explained to her the new socialist world order and she was thrilled. Those who could afford it bought modern furniture for the new apartment, for instance by the German Hellerau workshops near Dresden. – *Ein rauchendes Pärchen im gemeinsam durchkomponierten Wohnzimmer. Es scheint, als wolle er ihr die neue sozialistische Weltordnung erklären, und sie kann's kaum glauben. Zum Erstbezug in der Stalinallee leistete sich, wer konnte, moderne Möbel, etwa aus den Deutschen Werkstätten Hellerau bei Dresden.*

The first building completed on Stalinallee in 1951, on the occasion of the first World Festival of Youth and Students, was the Deutsche Sporthalle designed by the architect Richard Paulick. It was built in social classicist style over the period of only 148 days. The West German abutments planned for the construction could not be used because their delivery was denied at the last minute by the highest GDR authorities. A temporary roof construction and replacement abutments that were scattered inside the building, covering the view at events, were the cause of its closing down in 1968 due to danger of collapsing before it was torn down in 1972. The statues in front of the portal were modelled after the Schlüterhof of the recently demolished Berlin City Palace. — *Erster anlässlich der Weltjugendfestspiele fertiggestellter Bau in der Stalinallee im August 1951 war die in nur 148 Tagen im Stil des Sozialistischen Klassizismus errichtete Deutsche Sporthalle des Architekten Richard Paulick. Weil am Ende von oberster Stelle deren Lieferung abgelehnt wurde, durften die Stützpfeiler aus Westdeutschland nicht verbaut werden. Eine provisorische Dachkonstruktion und Ersatzpfeiler, die innerhalb des Gebäudes gestellt wurden und bei Veranstaltungen den Blick versperrten, waren ursächlich dafür, dass die Halle 1968 wegen Einsturzgefahr gesperrt und 1972 abgerissen wurde. Die Statuen vor der Frontfassade waren vom Schlüterhof des gerade abgerissenen deutschen Stadtschlosses adaptiert worden.*

1968

1959 / 65

The ambitiously modern second construction phase from 1959 to 1965 reaching from Strausberger Platz to Alexanderplatz; the Café Moskau was built in 1964 (Photo), the cinema Kino International in 1965: A picture of elegant gentlemen at happy hour; their view out the window shows the Kino International with the Berolina Hotel in the background. – *Von 1959 bis 1965 währte der ehrgeizig-moderne zweite Bauabschnitt vom Strausberger Platz Richtung Alexanderplatz. Es entstand 1964 das Café Moskau (linke Seite), 1965 wurde das Kino International fertig: Auf dem Foto befinden sich die eleganten Herrschaften in der Happy Hour, und wenn sie sich zum Fenster drehen, blicken sie hinüber zum Kino International mit dem Hotel Berolina im Hintergrund.*

1958 The towers at Frankfurter Tor are a so called real-socialistic interpretation of Schinkel's dome in Berlin's Mitte district. The picture shows how the boulevard was designed with very large green areas and relatively narrow lanes for cars. The street was explicitly not meant for urban traffic only but as the representative East German capital's prospekt for demonstrations and parades. – *Die Türme des Frankfurter Tores sollten die Schinkelschen Domkuppeln in Berlin-Mitte in erektiver Ausbildung würdigen und realsozialistisch interpretieren, aber dennoch überragend vereinnahmen als Sinnbild für das aufstrebende Proletariat. Schön zu erkennen die Gestaltung der Allee als überdurchschnittlich breiter Grünstreifen mit einer relativ schmalen Autostraße, die ausdrücklich nicht nur für den städtischen Verkehr vorgesehen war. Der Prospekt sollte Ostberlins Anspruch als repräsentative Hauptstadt mit Aufmarsch- und Paradestrecke gerecht werden.*

1961 Even the ten to twelve year old children were affected, consciously or not, by the consequences of the war. The safe new world of the Stalinallee was meant to facilitate a healthy growth in superficially proper conditions. The three girls must now be around 75-year-old ladies that have lived in peaceful times ever since. — *Auch die Zehn- bis Zwölfjährigen hatten Anfang der 50er-Jahre bewusst oder unbewusst die Folgen des Krieges zu verarbeiten. Die neue heile Welt der Stalinallee sollte gesunde Entwicklung in äußerlich geordneten Verhältnissen fördern. Die drei Mädchen sind heute um die 75 Jahre alte Damen und haben seit damals Frieden erlebt.*

ca. 1955

Sophisticated neon signs on shops would add international flair to the boulevard. The government increased public property through expropriation of private businesses. Nationally owned combines bundled those still existing by merging. The "Nationally Owned Automotive Manufacturing", liquidated already in the 1950s, turned into the IFA, the "Industrial Association of Automotive Manufacturing", hence the neon signs soon had to be removed again.   —   *Aufwendige Neon-Leuchtreklamen an den Geschäften sollten der Allee weltstädtisches Flair verleihen. Im Interesse der Regierenden lag unter anderem, das Volkseigentum durch Unternehmer-Enteignungen zu vermehren. In der Industrie entstanden sogenannte volkseigene Betriebe und Kombinate, die die noch vorhandenen Einzelunternehmen bündelten. Aus dem „Volkseigenen Fahrzeugbau", aufgelöst bereits Anfang der 50er-Jahre, entstand der IFA, der „Industrieverband Fahrzeugbau" – also musste der Neonschriftzug bald wieder abgebaut werden.*

View over Strausberger Platz up to the towers at Frankfurter Tor. The center still without a fountain, but with many parking lots. — *Blick über den Strausberger Platz bis zu den Türmen am Frankfurter Tor. Die Platzmitte noch ohne Brunnen, am Rand des Kreisels viele Parkmöglichkeiten.* 1956

2014 The fountain of the famous Berlin artisan metal worker Fritz Kühn was added to Strausberger Platz in 1967. It is made of ornamental wrought sculptural copper plates shaped like diamond cubes. The two 14-story towers "Haus des Kindes" and "Haus Berlin", unlike the rest of the brickwork at the square, were built with prefabricated parts of reinforced concrete. The "Haus Berlin" housed restaurants, cafés and bars while the "Haus des Kindes" offered a children's café on the topmost floor with a sign saying "Adults must be accompanied by a child". — Der Strausberger Platz erhielt 1967 den Brunnen des berühmten Berliner Metallkünstlers Fritz Kühn, gestaltet aus plastisch getriebenen Kupferplatten in Diamantquaderung als Ornament. Die beiden 14-geschossigen Türme „Haus des Kindes" und „Haus Berlin" wurden im Gegensatz zum gemauerten Rest des Platzes als Montagebauten aus Stahlbetonfertigteilen errichtet. Während im „Haus Berlin" Restaurants, Cafés und Bars untergebracht waren, gab es im „Haus des Kindes" im obersten Geschoss ein Kindercafé, an dessen Eingang der Hinweis „Erwachsene nur in Begleitung von Kindern" stand.

The corner house at Lichtenberger Straße is a paradigm for the "National Tradition" style with its modern silhouette and standing on a plain base of arcades. The decoration of ceramic stucco, friezes and colonnades on the roof represent Prussian classicism. This mix forms the "socialist classicism" that was demanded at that time. — *Das Eckhaus Lichtenberger Straße ist Paradigma für den Stil der „Nationalen Tradition"; in seiner Silhouette zwar modern und auf schnörkelloser Arkadensockelung, in den Dekorelementen allerdings durch Keramikstuck, Friese und Säulenkolonnaden auf dem Dach preußisch-klassizistisch staffiert. Dieser Mix bildet jene damals geforderte Form des „sozialistischen Klassizismus".*

2015 — The interplay of light and shadow on the towers at the entrance of the ensemble shines timeless and unchanged. — *Das Licht- und Schattenspiel auf den Türmen am Eingang des Ensembles strahlt zeitlos und unverändert.*

Rub and Smell
Berlin Past

THE SMELL OF ´HISTORY´

CLOSE YOUR EYES AND LET YOUR NOSE TAKE YOU ON A LITTLE TIME TRAVEL – THE NORWEGIAN SCIENTIST/ARTIST SISSEL TOLAAS MAKES IT POSSIBLE. – *DIE AUGEN SCHLIESSEN UND MIT DER NASE EINE KLEINE ZEITREISE MACHEN – DIE NORWEGISCHE WISSENSCHAFTLERIN UND KÜNSTLERIN SISSEL TOLAAS MACHT'S MÖGLICH.*

SMELL BY: SISSEL TOLAAS RE_SEARCHLAB BERLIN

Sissel Tolaas exceptional ability to replicate various smells has already amazed major brands like Mercedes Benz, Adidas and Louis Vuitton. Especially for this picture book, she has faithfully recreated the smell of Berlin – both from the era of the Wall and up to present day. BERLIN'S PAST emerges from years' worth of collected Berlin smell molecules. Rubbing gently on page 166 invokes an olfactory déjà-vu. The page on the right reveals BERLIN'S PRESENT with its unmistakable contemporary fragrance.

◇◇◇◇◇◇

Mit ihrer außergewöhnlichen Fähigkeit Gerüche nachzubilden, hat Sissel Tolaas bereits große Marken wie Mercedes Benz, Adidas oder Louis Vuitton verblüfft. Eigens für diesen Bildband hat sie den Duft Berlins zu Zeiten der Mauer und den Duft von heute nachempfunden: Mit über die Jahre gesammelten Berliner Duftmolekülen entstand BERLIN PAST. Durch Reiben wird Seite 166 zu einem olfaktorischen Déjà-vu. Auf der rechten Seite entfaltet dann BERLIN PRESENT seinen zeitgenössischen Duft.

Rub and Smell
Berlin Present

THE EDITORS / DIE AUTOREN

———◇◇◇◇◇◇◇◇◇◇◇———

Stephan Schilgen, born in 1967 in West Berlin, studied sociology and information science. Then he finally discovered the right location to implement his idea – a club that would appeal to the senses and simultaneously be a dance floor, theater, bar and restaurant, established in 1997.

As a result of the club's consistent style with its playful Op art installations, since 1998 the media and industry started to require the services of the club founder as designer, interior designer and contractor. At about the same time private clients also wanted interiors designed by him. Since then the company has grown to become a system that today accomplishes special design ideas for clients like Chanel and Bvlgari, but also engages in small substantial projects.

André M. Wyst was basically born as a whole-blooded designer in 1969, the year of the first manned moon landing. He researches subjects and contents, creates narratives and visual aesthetics. This interdisciplinary approach allowed him to work in style-defining ways for the jewel of the Condé Nast Publishing House, "Architectural Digest", from 2009 until the magazine's relocation to Munich in 2012. But moving to Bavaria was not an option for him: "As a native Berliner it is impossible to leave."

André contributed to the design-development of the art magazine "Monopol", "Zoo-Magazin", influenced the look of the Indie cover "Intersection" and creates luxury branding, corporate publishing and book designs for various publishing houses in germany.

—

Stephan Schilgen, geboren 1967 in Berlin (West), entdeckte nach dem Studium der Soziologie und Informationswissenschaften endlich den richtigen Ort, um seine Idee eines alle Sinne ansprechenden Clubs umzusetzen, der ab 1997 gleichzeitig Tanzladen, Bühne, Bar und Restaurant wurde.

Ab 1998 erhielt der Gründer, als Reaktion auf den konsequenten Look des Clubs mit seinen verspielt-digitalen Op-Art-Installationen, erste Aufträge von Industrie und Medien als Designer, Innenarchitekt und Bauleiter. Zeitgleich wollten sich private Kunden ihre Räume entwickeln und ausgestalten lassen. Und so wuchs das Unternehmen über die Jahre zu einem System, das heute für Kunden wie Chanel und Bvlgari besondere Ideen umsetzt, sich aber auch für kleine gehaltvolle Projekte engagiert.

André M. Wyst ist – im Grunde seit seiner Geburt im Jahr der Mondlandung 1969 – ein Vollblutgestalter. Er recherchiert Themen und Inhalte, entwickelt Erzählformen und Bildästhetiken. Dieser fachübergreifende Ansatz ermöglichte es ihm, beim Juwel des Condé Nast-Verlagshauses, bei „Architectural Digest", von 2009 bis zu deren Umzug 2012 nach München stilprägend zu arbeiten. Aber nach Bayern wollte er nicht: „Als gebürtiger Berliner kann ich hier unmöglich weg."

André wirkte bei der Design-Entwicklung des Kunstmagazins „Monopol", bei „Zoo"-Magazin, prägte den Look des Indie-Titels „Intersection", arbeitet an Luxury Branding, für Corporate Publishing und zeichnet für Buchgestaltungen bei diversen Verlagen verantwortlich.

Stephan Schilgen (left) in an apartment he designed in Berlin Charlottenburg

André M. Wyst in his apartment in Berlin-Mitte

IMPRINT / IMPRESSUM

This book was conceived and edited by STEPHAN SCHILGEN, ANDRÉ M. WYST

Publisher EINAR SKJERVEN, www.skjerven.com
Concept, Final artwork, Production TPA, Agentur für Kommunikationsdesign

Research, Text, Supervising by STEPHAN SCHILGEN
Additional research by GÜNTER HÖHNE
Translation by JULIA DORNAUER, CAROLINE DIETZ
Picture editing by KRISTIN LOSCHERT
Copy-editing and proofreading by BETTINA SCHNEUER

Art Direction and Design by ANDRÉ M. WYST

Photographer HANS-GEORG ESCH, MARTIN MAI, OLIVER MARK, ANDREAS GERKE, JENS BÖSENBERG, RINGO PAULUSCH

Smell by SISSEL TOLAAS RE_SEARCHLAB BERLIN

Exclusive worldwide distribution
Die Gestalten Verlag GmbH & Co. KG. Berlin
www.gestalten.com, sales@gestalten.com

ISBN 978-3-89955-578-3

None of the content in this book was published in exchange for payment by commercial parties or designers; we selected everything based solely on its artistic merit.

PICTURE INDEX / BILDNACHWEIS

BPK, BILDARCHIV PREUSSISCHER KULTURBESITZ
Bildagentur für Kunst, Kultur und Geschichte, bpk / Max Ittenbach

DEUTSCHES HISTORISCHES MUSEUM
Presse-Foto Röhnert / Deutsches Historisches Museum, Berlin
P.M. Olsen / Deutsches Historisches Museum, Berlin
Deutsches Historisches Museum, Berlin
Walter Womacka / Deutsches Historisches Museum / VG Bildkunst

OSTKREUZ, AGENTUR DER FOTOGRAFEN
Ludwig Schirmer/OSTKREUZ, Ute Mahler/OSTKREUZ,
Harald Hauswald/OSTKREUZ, Thomas Sandberg/OSTKREUZ

DPA, DEUTSCHE PRESSE-AGENTUR
picture alliance / akg-images, picture-alliance / Mary Evans / Grenville Collins P

All rights reserved. No part of this publication may be reproduced or transmitted in
any form or by any means, electronic or mechanical, including photocopy or any storage
and retrieval system, without permission in writing from the publisher.